Machine Learning for Beginners

Easy Guide of ML, Deep Learning, data analytics and Cyber Security in practice. Modern approach of Neural Networks, Predictive Modeling and Data Mining with 50 Key Terms

Table of Content

INTRODUCTION

Congratulations on purchasing *Machine Learning for Beginners,* and thank you for doing so. The future is predicted to utilize machine learning techniques to solve everyday situations, and downloading this book is the firsts step to act before it caught up with you. Since its incorporation in the 1950s, machine learning has a broad and complex concept which may become more challenging for beginners to venture. However, the initial step in understanding machine learning is usually the easiest and among those found in the following chapters.

The following chapters will, therefore, highlight the primary aspects of machine learning, which primarily the building blocks are. Beginning with the basics provides you with a clear idea of what machine learning is all about. Consequently, machine learning uses multiple terms which may become challenging or sometimes misunderstood, especially for beginners. In this case, the chapters will isolate these vocabularies while providing detailed information about what they stand for when it comes to machine learning.

When you are quite familiar with what machine learning is all about, including basics and terms used, the book will highlight the introduction to different concepts. As the book is primarily for beginners, understanding basics, as well as a brief and detailed introduction to different areas of machine learning, is essential. Besides, you will learn about the dos and don'ts of machine learning, algorithms of machine learning, and fundamental theories in this topic.

There are plenty of books on this subject on the market, thanks again for choosing this one! Every effort was made to ensure it is full of as much useful information as possible, please enjoy!

CHAPTER 1: FUNDAMENTAL CONCEPTS OF MACHINE LEARNING

"Machine learning is the science of getting computers to learn

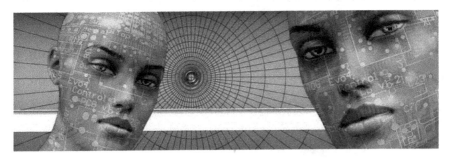

without being explicitly programmed"
Sebastian Thrun

Basics of Machine Learning

Machine learning is described as the ability for machines to understand human behavior and speech autonomously from experience, analysis, and observation tessellation based on specific data without programming. When compared to machine learning, programming entails writing a set of given codes or programs and inputting explicit instruction where the computer or machine follows to perform a given task. Whereas, machine learning depends on a data set where the device readily identifies and analyzes the data set and make decisions without any external assistance.

These machines would, therefore, perform a given task automatically when they observe and learn from the dataset without being fed more similar instructions. Machine learning covers a broader field of computing. As such, beginners should expect several courses or articles to cover these topics fully. For example, Facebook uses machine learning to such as facial recognition algorithm to quickly identify an individual; therefore, users can tag photos when uploaded. Another example is Google Voice Service used in multiple smartphones where people can readily use voice search assistance.

How Machines Learn

Machines have been made to observe, learn, and analyze different functions and events like how humans do. The first concept of machine learning began in 1943, where neural networks of the human brain were introduced to computers. However, the development of computing devices, both hardware, and software, at the time was slow and solely used in large organizations and academic institutions. More so, acquiring the necessary data was difficult, unlike the current days where we quickly access the internet and get what we need.

Humans acquire the knowledge about a given thing, memorize it and retrieve it in the time of need when a similar occurrence occurs in the future. This behavior is conducted by a network of neurons in the brain. The same pattern was introduced to machines making them work like how brains recognize different features and distinguish them at different times in the future when they arise. Machine learning can also take various forms when computers learn. That is, some may become specific and perform a given task while others are general learning multiple topics and implementing them like how our brains work.

Basic Terms Commonly Used in Machine Learning

Bias

Bias is a term used in machine learning to describe the model developed either if the predictability level is low or high. That is, if the bias is low, then the machine has a much higher predictability level with an increased biasness suggesting a lower predictability level. Therefore, biasness in machine learning tends to determine the level of mistakes made when executing datasets. The primary benefit of bias in machine learning is that it readily provides a comparison of algorithms between two machines if the problems are alike.

Cross-Validation Bias

This is a term used to suggest a technique used in machine learning to measure the accuracy of performance of the model. Cross-validation bias usually provides the performance relatively closer to the intended outcome, primarily when the model is used in the future without the primary dataset. This technique utilizes the present knowledge fed to predict future unseen situations. When provided with the correct model, cross-validation bias can result in much higher performance.

Underfitting and Overfitting

Underfitting is a term typically used to describe events where the machine learning models are unable to predict the intended dataset with the required level of accuracy. There are several reasons which may result in these situations, for instance, when you fail to collect the right features or on complex problem statements. On the other hand, overfitting is when the model fits excessively or becomes too complicated also used in statistics. Here, the machine learns in detail and much more profound than expected; therefore, the outcome, though positive, may impact the performance negatively.

Deep Learning, Machine Learning, and Artificial Learning

Beginners may face a challenge when trying to differentiate between machines, artificial and deep learning when it comes to machine learning. Artificial learning comprises of tools which simulate how we behave and make decisions intelligently like us. Machine learning, as mentioned, is the ability of machines to learn automatically without programming using codes or programs. Deep learning combines both artificial and machine learning but with the assistance of algorithms and artificial neural networks.

Components of Machine Learning

Data Collection and Preparation

Machines can never work unless fed with the relevant data which triggers the application of the intended task. The first step in machine learning is collecting and preparing data which is divided into training and testing data. An example is when you want to create software which quickly identifies photos of specific persons. First, collect the data of the people, intended and set your parameters based on age, sex, or other relevant information and input your data on a model which can be tested.

Selection and Training of Models

Choosing your model and training it depending on your requirements as another essential component which determines the outcome of your machine learning strategy. However, several algorithms and models of machine learning incorporated have undergone modification to provide solutions to problems at hand. Choose a model which can be readily trained to fit your criterion for your machine to understand and provide solutions immediately.

Model Evaluation

When a given data is fed into a machine, it readily learns features and patterns of the data train itself to work like how to learn new things. More so, when fed a well-tested data, machines can produce excellent results when deciding on their own. As to achieve this, work on the training data which will eventually create a model for your computer. The model would provide an algorithm where the device will follow, therefore providing higher chances of success. Then test the data to ascertain its probability of delivering excellent results at the end.

Types of Machine Learning Algorithms

Supervised Algorithms

Supervised machine learning algorithms are data sets which consist of input parameters and intended outcome labeled within the machine. Here, the machine classifies data sets into labels, and the training data included according to the given parameters. The features and patterns will be readily read and classified as intended depending on the learning capabilities of the machine. This type of machine learning algorithm can further be classified into two forms, classification and regression algorithms.

Classification algorithms are primarily responsible for classifying data into a specific label or categories with one of the most commonly used being the K-Nearest Neighbor classification algorithm. The K-Nearest classification algorithm is primarily used for classifying data depending on the similarities between different data sets. Regression algorithms, on the other hand, are specifically essential in the determination of mathematical relationship and dependency between variables. Regression algorithms can, therefore, be used to predict the outcome and also include two forms, linear and logistic recession, which determine the equations used.

Unsupervised Algorithms

Unlike supervised machine learning algorithms, unsupervised algorithms entail unlabeled data sets classified in the form of similarities of variables given. Some of the most used unsupervised algorithms include K-means clustering, recurrent, and artificial neural network. The K-means clustering machine learning algorithm entails formations of clusters or groups of similar and related data sets. Artificial neural networks are successive artificial neurons identical to that of the brain connected with nodes for the benefit of making machines think and operate as humans. While recurrent neural networks are a type of artificial neural network which uses a memory connected to its nodes for analyzing sequential data.

Reinforcement Algorithms

Among the types of machine learning is the reinforced machine learning algorithm, which makes a machine to determine ideas specifically within a given context. This algorithm is quite beneficial, especially when it comes to maximizing the outcome though it also takes risks as chances of punishments are extensive. In this case, the machine becomes aware of the mistake and make corrections; hence, most of the time, the results will become positive. Besides, you can readily program or modify the outcome to either be long-term or short-term under the Markov Decision Process.

CHAPTER 2: APPLICATION OF MACHINE LEARNING

"We need to be vigilant about how we design and train these machine-learning systems, or we will see ingrained forms of bias built into the artificial intelligence of the future"
Kate Crawford

Understanding about machine learning has crucial benefits that sitting on your computer and creating dataset models. Since its introduction into the computing world, machine learning has gained much popularity among developers and users, therefore, applied in different areas. Machine learning application range from small technological devices to more large machinery used commercially. Some of the areas used include social media such as Facebook, Twitter, and Instagram where it used for the analysis of sentiments and filtering spam, as well as in the transport sector especially in safety monitoring and traffic control. Others areas include e-commerce, health, financial services, visual assistant, and trading mainly on Algorithm Trading.

How Machine Learning Can Improve Our Society

Machine learning has a lot of potentials to impact the everyday life of humans, therefore essential in building our societies with the provision of solutions to recurring challenges. Despite being seen as a substitute to most of the human doings, machine learning accompanies different ways of how society is predicted to have developed by use of these computer learning abilities.

Healthcare

As already seen in most developed and some developing countries, the use of modem techniques of providing treatment has grown significantly. For instance, microscopic and challenging diagnosis of certain conditions may become a challenge for most doctors. In this case, the use of machine learning algorithms has the potential to learn how spotting abnormalities during analysis is done and be able to utilize the same knowledge to simplify this problem. As such, machines can be fed with models which relate to health specialists techniques and use the experience to readily impact the society positively and provide a solution to small and complicated medical conditions.

Transport

The world today is full of vehicles which are filling our highways and demand for the control for the benefit of allowing for safety and prevention of traffics. Therefore, the transport sector has, to some extent, already utilizing machine learning on the roads to guarantee safety and control of traffic. For instance, we have seen sensors on roads and rails to allow the smooth running of the sector. Besides, today, most cars, buses, and trucks use computers for different purposes, including navigation. The same has been adopted in ships, airplanes, and trains used around the world. Self-driving is also on the rise with vehicles being able to maneuver without the need of a steering wheel or someone to manage vehicle, train, ship or plane controls.

Education

VR and AR have been adopted in teaching learners about different aspects without necessarily leaving the classroom. For instance, children can easily explore the world using digital maps while in one room, therefore, making them understand different countries without actually visiting them. In the near future, scientists predict that machine learning will play a significant role in providing education to children, especially when using machines controlled by a teacher to individual students. As such, machine learning will ensure individual students are curated with courses where they are struggling henceforth promoting their academic status.

Retail

Machine learning has already played a role in the e-commerce sector, and that is expected to grow and promote the retail industry. Provision of meaningful data and insights of a given business, especially for customers, will readily encourage the growth of retail stores. Despite some suggesting that the retail sector will die due to the rise of machine learning, others oppose and indicate that will flourish with technologies like facial recognition as well as personalized customer experiences in stores.

Entertainment

With no doubt, the entertainment sector has already witnessed the benefits of machine learning despite not in the intended levels. For example, new technologies such as lights, sounds, and motions created by CGI advancements have significantly impacted the sector. Movies have, therefore showed remarkable benefit from machine learning. The same has been seen in sports, music and gaming industries with the benefit of making these devices and enjoyable moments more reliable, ease of access and effective. Machines learning are, therefore expected to revolutionize the entertainment sector and benefit the general community.

When to Avoid the Use of Machine Learning

Machine learning is a broad technological aspect which may also become very dangerous when misused. That is, when you feed your machine with irrelevant data, the chances are that the device would both learn profoundly and explore the unwanted facts or rather fail to perform. For example, a machine may opt to learn about war and eventually become too bias and learn more about killings and destruction. When such instances happen, it may simulate the same and engage in sabotage, therefore, leading to disaster.

Some of the instances to avoid the introduction of machine learning include planning and creation of datasets for a machine without data scientists, beginning the process with irrelevant data, poor infrastructure of machine learning and implementation of real datasets without proper strategy. Other cases may include mistakes on your objectives, splitting data incorrectly, and lack of modification on hidden variables. There are other significant mistakes which can be found before or during the development of machine learning procedures. In this case, you should avoid the use of machine learning, especially when implementing it to large populations.

Paradigms of Machine Learning

Supervised Machine Learning

Like mentioned above, supervised machine learning entails learning techniques of machines but within given parameters, more so, supervised learning. The input and output variables are provided a mapping to show how they relate, therefore having a managed outcome. Supervised machine learning offers the ability to readily approximate mapping functions too quickly so that new data can be inserted without altering but predicting the output variable. Supervised learning is quite like a teacher who supervises the learning of students, and any answers provided can be moderated or iterated by the teacher.

Supervised learning usually remains active until when the whole process stops after achieving the intended level of performance. Supervised learning is classified into classification learning where the problems are categorized based on similarities, and regression learning is when the output is a real value. Common examples of machine learning include linear regression, random forest, and support vector machines.

Unsupervised Machine Learning

The same has also been mentioned where unsupervised learning comprises of input data only without the probability of predicting output variables. The primary goal of unsupervised learning is to enable modeling of the structure of the dataset and learn more about the outcome. Here, the machine has no correct answer or a teacher like in supervised learning. Algorithms, therefore, work on their own to evaluate and provide rewards for their analysis. Unsupervised can be classified into clustering learning where you determine a natural grouping of data and association learning to discover relations between big data.

Reinforcement Learning

Reinforcement learning is used in several disciplines apart from machine learning more so in operation research, where it is referred to as approximate dynamic programming. In machine learning, reinforcement learning is mainly concerned with software agents and how their impacts affect the outcome of cumulative reward. It is among the three paradigms of machine learning bit differs from supervised and unsupervised machine learning. Reinforcement is usually used in machine learning to maximize the outcome of a given dataset.

An example of reinforcement learning is a puzzle where an agent has to go through different paths with an objective of finding a free means of reaching the reward without meeting obstacles. The machines, in this case as the agent, learn how to maneuver while avoiding obstacles, therefore, reaching the reward. That is, the machine will try different means with the right moves giving it a positive reward and a wrong or meeting an obstacle offering a negative reward. Therefore, reinforcement learning entails input, output, training, and continuous learning of the machine.

Data Science and Machine Learning

Data science is a multidisciplinary field of study which encompasses data inference, technology, algorithm development as well as scientific methods and systems to generate knowledge and insights useful in the solving analytical sophisticated structural and unstructured data problems. The primary goal of data science is determining findings from the general data with an effort of providing solutions to daily occurrences in different fields of science. The discovered data insights are usually quantitative essential for decision making businesses as well as data products which include algorithm solutions and operational scale.

Data science and machine learning have significant interaction, especially machine learning, which provides vital methodologies to data science. In this case, machine learning develops algorithms used by data scientists to create more for the creation of knowledge and insights for solving problems. On the other hand, machine learning significantly depends on data science which has the necessary data used to create algorithms essential for the machine to learn and work separately. Therefore, both data science and machine learning depend on each other, more so in regression, supervised clustering, and Naïve Bayes.

Machine Learning Algorithms

Linear Regression

This is a type of supervised learning which involves both input and output variables being determined. In a linear regression algorithm, the relationship between variables is expressed in the form of an equation, that is, $y = a + bx$. The primary function of linear regression is, therefore, determining the value of a and b provided that y and x are known. Linear regression algorithms are used in statistics, especially in population census and measuring of rainfall in cm.

Logistics Regression Algorithm

This is another type of supervised machine learning where the input variable is known, but the output remains unknown. The prediction is usually discrete, unlike a linear regression algorithm, more so when introduced with a transformational function. Logistics regression is quite suited in a binary classification where datasets take the form of y = 1 or 0 with 1 being the default class. However, when the transformation function is introduced, the regression is termed as logistic function h(x) = 1/ (1 + ex) forming an S-shaped curve on a graph. Logistics regression algorithm is more so used in unpredictable data sets such as learning association like whether students are going to pass or fail in an examination.

Decision Tree

Decision tree also referred to as Classification and Regression Tree (CART), use nodes which represent input and output variables. The model is quite unique and uses multiple nodes; for example, nonterminal nodes represent input variables while leaf variables are for outputs. The decision tree is essential in creating probabilities of the future with the form. For example, one can use the tree to determine if you can buy a car in the event of another need which is also crucial. In this case, decision trees are beneficial to the prediction of future events, especially in the mining sector.

Support-Vector Machine (SVM)

This is another form of supervised machine learning algorithm of data analysis essential for classification and regression analysis. SVM assigns more variables to a given context with similar or related data, therefore, making it non-probabilistic binary linear classifier. The categories are separated by a clear and reasonable gap for ease of identification of differences. SVM are conventional solvers of modern problems and widely used in biological and related sciences, image classification, text and hypertext classification and recognition of handwriting patterns.

Naïve Bayes

The Naïve Bayes provides an algorithm where you can readily calculate the occurrence of an event when another has already happened. This supervised learning uses the Bayes theorem, which uses dependent and independent variables which determine the existence of the event. Naïve Bayes is mostly used as a weather forecasting tools as it predicts the coming events based on the previous happenings of the weather.

K-Nearest Neighbor Algorithm (KNN)

KNN is another machine learning algorithm which uses an entire dataset as a single training set and test set for a given computer. When retrieving the data needed, KNN uses dataset as a whole to find the K-nearest variable to the new event or those similar to the variable. The outcome or reward is usually averaged, and the results portray a mean or model which solves the problem at hand. KNN is generally applied in situations where you are searching for similar files such as in semantical documents and recommender systems.

K-Means Algorithms

This is unsupervised learning which groups similar data into clusters and calculates k value of centroids which gives the clusters a considerable distance between clusters. Initially, you will have to choose the value of k then assign each data point and compute to obtain clusters matching the value assigned k. Assign points between cluster centroids on each group and calculate the correct distance between them. Besides, ensure there exists not switching of points. K-means are most suited during clustering of big datasets and successfully used in astronomy, market segmentation, and vector quantization.

Random Forest

Random forest entails several decision trees represented by a multitude of nodes which suggests input and output variables. Random forest algorithms are created when multiple models are connected to develop a massive connection of trees of datasets, therefore, referred to as a forest. The trees are initially sampled to obtain the similarity and then connected with through nodes. Some of the applications of random decision forest algorithm include diagnosis of faults in machines such as engines as well as in the health industry to determine problems in diabetic retinopathy.

The Buildings Blocks of Machine Learning Algorithms

Machine learning uses applied mathematical basics, especially in the development of algorithms used in both supervised and unsupervised learning as well as reinforcement learning. More so, these algorithms use scalars vectors, matrices, and tensor to create variables which are interconnected in different forms and bring out the machine learning models. The general term algorithm signifies several mathematics applications derived from different areas.

Tensor, for instance, is a topic in mathematics which primarily deals with an algebraic object similar to vectors but double spaced and may take multiple forms. Another primary component of machine algorithm is scalar, or scalar quantity both used in mathematics and physics derived from single elements and has magnitude. Vectors are the most essential applied in multiple areas with both magnitude and direction and may include algebra and connected to other algebraic expressions or objects. Lastly are matrices comprising of rectangular arrays, expressions, numbers or symbols organized in rows and columns. The four are considered the primary building blocks of machine learning algorithms giving machines the ability to simulate human behaviors effectively.

Deep Learning and Cognitive Computing

As mentioned, deep learning is the broader machine learning method and comprises of artificial neural learning and machine learning on both supervised and unsupervised machine learning algorithms. Deep learning, therefore, consists of deep, recurrent, and convolutional neural networks. On the other hand, cognitive computing is where the machine applies the knowledge gained from cognitive science to create the architecture of several artificial Intelligence subsystems, including machine learning and human-computer interaction.

Like machine learning, both deep learning and cognitive computing use algorithms which alter the functions of how programming and coding functions giving the machine a new form of how to perform without human interaction. When correct datasets of variables have been fed into the computer, it readily incorporates the information and begins to learn on how to act on such events and develop inclusions without interaction to human. Therefore, several machine learning methods have become successful with machines now being able to respond and create things without inputting specific dataset parameters.

Basic Statistics and Probability Theory

Statistics and probability may have broader differences between them in mathematics, but when it comes to machine learning, they have several similarities. However, they do have dissimilarities depending on the algorithms used in each model. Probability is a fundamental aspect of machine learning and has been used to refer to the possibility of occurrences between happenings of two events. The prospect has always been termed to have values between 0 and 1. However, machine learning changes this narrative to ascertain that we can actually understand the outcome of a possibility when we jaw the right measurements.

When it comes to statistical data, a similar aspect can be adopted, but machine learning also depends on statistics which enables the process of classifying similar data more so on supervised learning algorithms. The theory behind statistics and probability of machine learning suggests that machines not only learn and remember the same event in the future but also utilize the probabilistic approach to determine if the event can occur again. The statistical theory indicates that machined considerably group data in the form which build an organized type of data for quick retrieval.

Deep Learning for Intelligent Agents

Deep learning, as stated, is the most comprehensive form of machine simulation and the most effective when it comes to machine learning. Since the introduction of deep learning, it has been used in the most complex and extensive areas with the benefit of effectiveness. When mentioning about deep learning intelligent agents, deep learning works as a machine which gather information regularly or when instructed by the user in real-time. An intelligent agent is therefore described as a program, usually a bot, which can make decisions or take actions depending on its surroundings, experience, or as instructed.

For example, games are developed daily with algorithms which utilize deep learning to either control or enhance the play. However, deep learning is used to act as intelligent agents to create more benefits to the game, especially for the game to respond to human interaction. When games become more interactive, so does the play become more interesting. In this case, the intelligent agent built within the game can make decisions and perform tasks or moves with the aim of defeating the player. Another form of an intelligent agent is used in the finance sector, where they readily react to the market value. That is, when selling your property or trading, prices or points may either shoot or drop henceforth affecting your indicated value. Therefore, intelligent agents play a significant role in moving with the trend where it readily modifies your value depending on the market changes.

Technical Requirements of Deep Learning

Keras

Keras is an in build Python library created by Francois Chollet with the aim of facilitating immediate experimentations. The library can run along with TensorFlow and Theano, among others and supports several neural networks, including convolution, recurrent, and dense layers. Keras is essential in machine learning, as it enables different methods, including translation, speech, image, and face recognition. Some of the benefits include fast and straightforward prototypes, built-in support for multiple GPU training and has fully configurable modules, among others.

TensorFlow

This is the most common open-source libraries created by Google and essential for numerical computation. TensorFlow is written in C++ and Python and excellent in sophisticated events, for instance, during the creation of numerous neural networks more so on random decision trees. The algorithms used in the library provide room for voice and image recognition as well as text-to-speech applications. Some of the benefits of TensorFlow are multiple documentations and guidelines, support of distributed training and model serving and recommended by a large community of developers and tech firms.

PyTorch

PyTorch replaced the Torch library of Python and is written in Lua competing significantly with TensorFlow. This library was created by Facebook and used in top facilities such as the University of Oxford and Salesforce. PyTorch is mainly used for training deep learning algorithms and used may accompany a more significant percentage of researchers. Some of the benefits of PyTorch are modeling process quite direct and transparent, supports distributed training, model micro-services, direct embedding, and portable tools for development enhancements.

Examples of Deep Learning

Automotive Researchers

As mentioned, deep learning has gained popularity in the automotive sector, especially with the ability for engines to self-drive without human interaction. Deep learning in vehicles, trains, ships, and airplanes have been on the increase without human help control. You only sit and use your voice for the engine to start and move. These automotive are fitted with sensors, navigation, and other parameters which ascertain their movements without causing accidents or other related harm.

Medical Research

There have been numerous studies conducted to prevent, cure, and eliminate the dangers of cancer which are on the rise. As such, cancer researchers are utilizing deep learning to automatically detect cancer cells more so when they start building up for easy identification and elimination. In one instance, the UCLA team created a modern microscope which provides high-dimensional data, therefore, providing training of deep learning detect cancer cells.

Aerospace and Defense

Deep space has also been introduced in aerospace and defense, providing multiple benefits to these areas. For instance, deep learning enables astronauts and related researchers such as at NASA to detect objects caught by satellites readily. In defense, deep learning has played a significant role in mapping areas where troops are to visit and determine if they are safe or unsafe, therefore preventing the loss of soldiers in military missions.

CHAPTER 3: DATA ANALYTICS

"I stay away from the arts... writing songs, being creative - those are downloads from God. You can't do data analytics on art"

Troy Carter

In this chapter, you will learn about the concepts of data analytics and its application in Artificial Intelligence (AI) and Machine Learning (ML). You will also learn about the different types of Data Analytics as well as the differences between a data analyst and a business analyst. Read on to find out!

Definition of Data Analytics

Data Analytics (DA) refers to the process of examining sets of data to determine the information they contain with the help of highly specialized software and systems. Data analytics techniques are popularly applied in commercial industries to enable companies to make more informed decisions. Scientists and/or researchers also apply it to approve or disapprove theories, scientific models, and hypotheses.

Data analytics, as a term, refers to an assortment of applications, from reporting and online analytical processing (OLAP), basic business intelligence (BI) to different types of advanced analytics. The expensive use of the term, however, isn't universal although in some cases, the term data analytics is used by people to specifically mean advanced analytics treating Business Intelligence (BI) as a different entity.

Having known what data analytics is, let's look at the various types of data analytics.

Types of Data Analytics

Raw data can easily be compared to crude oil. Nowadays, anyone or any institution with a reasonable budget can collect huge volumes of raw data, but the collection should not be the end goal. Companies and institutions that can be able to get extra meanings from the raw data collected are the ones that can compete in the modern day's complex business environment. At the heart of data collection and seats a very important phenomenon: data analytics. It is what makes the entire process have importance.

There are various types of data analytics, as explained below, read on to find out!

1. Descriptive Analytics

The major focus of descriptive analytics is summarizing what happened in an organization or institution. It examines the raw data to answer different questions like what is happening? What happened? and what will happen?

Data analytics is characterized by business intelligence and visuals like pie charts, bar charts, line graphs, or generated narratives. An illustration of data analytics can be determining credit risk in a bank or supermarket. In such a scenario, previous financial performances can be carried out to foretell the client's financial performance.

Data analytics help provide insights into the sales cycle, like categorizing customers based on their history and preferences.

2.Diagnostic Analytics

Just as its name suggests, diagnostic analytics is applied in determining why something happened. For instance, when conducting a social media marketing campaign, you might want to access the number of reviews, followers, likes, and mentions after the campaign. Diagnostic analytics helps you filter numerous mentions into a single view; it breaks down the entire information to simple bits that you can comprehend within a few seconds.

3.Prescriptive Analytics

As other data analytics gives you general insights on a certain subject, prescriptive analytics provides you with laser-like focus in answering questions. For example, in the health industry, prescriptive analytics can be used to manage the patient population by determining the number of patients who are obese clinically.

It allows you to add filters in obesity like diabetes and cholesterol levels in order to find out areas the treatment should be focused.

4.Exploratory Analytics

This is an analytical approach that primarily focuses on establishing general patterns in raw data so as to identify features and outlines that might not have been discovered using other analytical methods. To use this approach, you must understand where outliers are occurring and the way different variables are related to making well-informed decisions.

For instance, in biological monitoring of data, websites might be affected by different stressors. Therefore, stressor correlations are very important when you try to relate the biological response variables and stressor variables. Scatterplots and correlation coefficients provide you comprehensive information on the relationship between the involved variables.

When analyzing different variables, however, the basic ways of multivariate visualization need to provide deeper insights.

5. Predictive Analytics

This is the use of machine learning techniques, data, and statistical algorithms to determine the probability of future results basing on historical data. The primary agenda of predictive analytics is helping you go beyond what as happened and give the most logic assessment of what is more likely going to happen in the future.

It uses recognizable results to come up with a model that can predict figures of different types of data as well as new data. Using recognizable results is important because it gives predictions that represent the likelihood of the targeted variable based on the estimated significance from the provided set of variables.

Predictive analytics can be applied in the banking systems to establish fraud cases, maximize the cross-sell and up-sell opportunities in a company, and measuring levels of credit risks.

This will help retain valuable clients to your business.

6. Mechanistic Analytics

Just as its name suggests, mechanistic analytics enable big data researchers to comprehend and understand clear alterations in procedures that can result in changing of variables. Equations in physical sciences and engineering determine the outcome of mechanistic analytics. They also allow data scientists to determine the parameters if they understand the equation.

7. Causal Analytics

They allow big data researchers to figure out what can happen if a single component of the variable is changed. When you opt for this approach, you should rely on the number of variables to determine what is going to happen next. The approach is appropriate if you're dealing with extremely large volumes of data.

8. Inferential Analytics

Inferential analytics takes different theories into account to determine certain aspects of the large population. When you use this approach, you will need to take a smaller sample of information from the target population and use it as a basis to infer parameters about the rest of the population.

After looking at the various types of data analytics, it is time you learned how data analytics is applied in different aspects. Read on to find out!

Data Analytics Application

Data analytics methodologies include The Exploratory Data Analysis (EDA) that aims to establish patterns in data and the Confirmatory Analysis (CDA) which uses statistical techniques in determining whether hypotheses about a certain set of data are false or true. While EDA is usually compared to detective work, CDA is similar to the task of a judge during a court trial.

Data analytics can be separated into Qualitative data analysis and Quantitative data analysis. Qualitative data analysis focuses on understanding the content of non-numerical data like images and audios. Quantitative data analysis, on the other hand, involves analyzing numerical data with quantifiable variables that can be measured statistically.

Data analytics can be applied in providing business executives and corporate workers with information about business operations, key performance indicators, customers, among others. This is done through BI and reporting. Previously, data reports and queries were mainly created for end users by BI developers, but today, organizations are increasingly using self-service BI tools let executives, business analysts as well as operational workers run their quarries and come up with reports by themselves.

Advanced types of data analytics include data mining: this involves going through large sets of data to identify patterns, trends, and relationships: Predictive analytics that seeks to predict customer behavior and machine learning: an AI technique that automated algorithms to sort through data set quicker than it can be done through conventional analytical modeling. Therefore, big data scientists apply data mining, predictive analytics, as well as machine learning to sets of big data that contain structured and semi-structured data. Text mining also provides a means of analyzing emails, documents, and other text-based content.

Data analytics have a wide range of business use. For instance, credit card companies and banks can analyze withdrawal and expenditure patterns to detect theft and prevent fraud.

Commercial companies and other marketing services providers do clickstream analysis so as to identify website viewers that are more likely to buy a product or service based on navigation and page-viewing sequence.

In addition, mobile network operators can examine customer data to forecast churn in order to prevent defections to rivals and boost customer relations. They also engage other companies in analyzing CRM analytics in order to fragment customers for marketing campaigns and equip their call centers with up-to-date information about callers. In healthcare, data analytics has also been used by organizations to mine patient data in order to evaluate the effectiveness of treatments to diseases such as cancer, AIDS, among others.

What Role Does Data Analytics Play in AI And ML?

Artificial Intelligence refers to the general field of algorithms in which machine learning is the leading inventory at the moment. AI is just a computer that has the ability to mimic or simulate human behavior or thought. Within that, there is a subset known as Machine Learning (ML) which is the most exciting part of Artificial Intelligence.

So how do ML, AI, and data analytics intercept?

ML is a branch of AI where a class of data-driven algorithms enables software applications to produce highly accurate data without any need of explicit programming.

The basic factor here is to build algorithms that can receive input data and induce statistical models to predict an outcome.

Data analytics employs science disciplines like mathematics and incorporates techniques like cluster analysis, data mining, and machine learning.

So, machine learning is a subset of AI, while data analytics is an interdisciplinary field used to extract meaning from data.

What Is the Difference Between A Data Analyst and A Business Analyst?

People often confuse between data analysts and business analysts. In some occasions, the two words are used to mean the same thing which shouldn't be the case. To find out the difference, let's look at each one of them and find out what it means.

Business Analyst

They do a lot of things in the business world. Their role primarily centers around requirement analysis. Some of the tasks business analysts do are; understanding genuine issues of stakeholders or business users, elicit and document business requirement, ensure completeness of business requirements, ensure that the technology team has comprehended the functionalities and is headed in the right direction.

Data Analyst

A data analyst manages to analyze large volumes of data, modeling data with the intention of coming up more useful business insights. The data analyst comes up with behavioral patterns and hypothesis on the primary basis of predictive analytics to support decision making.

They frequently utilize factual statistical models to make decisions and hypothesis.For instance, data analysis engages a lot of consumer-driven franchise and propelling their strategic business decisions. Subsequently, the outcome of data analytics forms the input of business decisions and essentially, how the system should be designed to suit those decisions. The driving factors of customer behavior or pattern, the designing systems these patterns are based on is governed by the efforts of a data analyst.

Although business analysts define the functionalities of the system, they solve issues by initiating the right feature in the system.

Skills wise, both data analysis and business analysis have contrasts and some comparability. Some of the skills needed for both roles are analytical mind, creating opportunities, the ability to see the master plan, a good business acumen, and presentation aptitude.

Both roles have an extraordinary future and bring a unique set of value to the table. A large number of organizations use both terms reciprocally and see them as the same. As seen from the above tasks and skills, they are quite different.

With more consumer data being accessible, data analysts have the upper hand in influencing the lives of people and make a difference to businesses and analytical business insights.

So, the answer to whether data analysts and business are the same no, you've seen the difference!

Qualitative and Quantitative Techniques

In data analytics, qualitative and quantitative analysis are two fundamental ways of data collection and interpretation. These methods can be used concurrently since they both have similar objectives. They might have some errors. So using them at the same time can make up for the errors each method has, leading to quality results.

There are overlaps in qualitative and quantitative analysis. I have outlined the similarities and differences between these two analyses techniques used in data analytics.

What is Quantitative Analysis?

This research analysis method is often associated with the numerical analysis where data is assembled, classified, and recorded for certain findings using a set of different methods. In this technique, data is chosen randomly in large samples and then comprehensively analyzed. The advantage when using quantitative analysis is that findings can be used and applied in a general population using the research patterns identified and developed in the sample. This is a disadvantage of qualitative data analysis because of limited generalizations of findings.

Quantitative analysis is objective. It aims to comprehend the occurrence of events and describe them using analytical methods. More clarity can, however, be obtained by concurrently using quantitative and qualitative techniques.

Quantitative analysis is mainly concerned measurable entities like length, width, temperature, weight, speed, and many more. Data can be represented in tabulated form, pie chart, line graph, or any other diagrammatic representation. Quantitative data can be categorized as either continuous or discrete, and it's often obtained using surveys, interviews, experiments, or observations.

There are limitations in quantitative analysis. For example, it can be difficult to discover new concepts using quantitative analysis and is where you need to apply qualitative analysis technique.

What is Qualitative Analysis?

It is concerned with analyzing data that can't be quantified. Qualitative analysis is about understanding the concepts of properties and attributes objects or participants. It gets a deeper understanding of "why" a certain phenomenon takes place. This analysis technique can be applied concurrently with quantitative analysis. Qualitative data can be wide-ranged and multi-faced, unlike quantitative analysis that is restricted by certain rules or numbers. When applying qualitative analysis, you must be well-rounded which any physical properties the study is based on.

The typical data analyzed qualitatively include gender, color, nationality, appearance, taste, among others, as long as they can't be computed. Such kind of data can be obtained through interviews.

Just like quantitative analysis, qualitative analysis has limitations. For example, it can't be used to generalize the entire population. Only small samples are applied in unstructured approach, and they do not represent the general population; hence, this method cannot be applicable in generalizing the entire population.

The qualitative data analysis technique is anchored on the classification of participants according to attributes and properties, while quantitative analysis is based on the classification of data anchored on computable values. Quantitative analysis is objective while qualitative analysis is subjective.

Therefore, there is a clear cutline between the two. They are both applied in data analytics, making it more accurate and credible.

Data analytics plays a significant role in today's world. You have learned of the different types of data analytics, how it is applied in various fields like AI, ML, and banking. Towards the end, you found out the difference between a data analyst and business analyst, the roles each one plays and features that distinguish them.

CHAPTER 4: NEURAL NETWORK

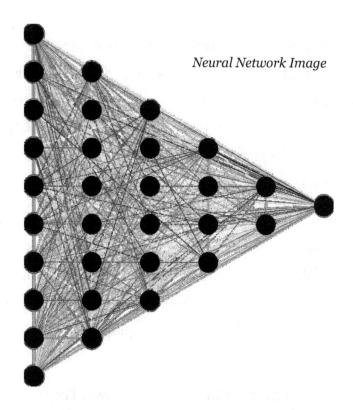

Neural Network Image

"The pooling operation used in convolutional neural networks is a big mistake, and the fact that it works so well is a disaster"
Geoffrey Hinton

A neural network is in simple terms described as either a software or hardware system programed to mimic the neurons found in human brains. The idea of neural network originated from two Chicago university researchers, namely Walter Pitts and Warren McCullough. It's several processors brought together to solve underlying issues in a series of trial and error. The idea of the neural network was majorly researched on different fields such as in technology and neuroscience sector in the early 1960s. The industry has recovered from its decline and is enjoying massive support in the technological world due to the modern era graphic chips. The chips have very high processing power disposal.

The neural network technology is applicable in different sectors fueling its resurgence. It is used in the analysis of a survey of oil, climate forecasting, and data analysis.

Neural Network Mathematics

Introduction

The idea of calculations involved in the neural network is not hard to work out; it all depends on the will, determination, and passion one employees. Most of the math in neuron network comprises of matrices.

1) Weights

Weights are the determination of neurons that transmit value. The size of the weight and value are directly proportional to each other. When the value being sent is low, then the weight is likely to be small and vice versa. The weight arranged in a matrix layout for calculation purposes. The neuron is usually placed in the input side.

For instance, an input layer which contains four neurons, and the subsequent layer contains five neurons. From this layout, a matrix can be formed of 4 rows and five columns. The weight values are then placed in the created matrix. The matrix can be named **P1** for easy identification. When there are different layers, then other matrices are formed with the same outline.

When a layer **P** contains **Y** neurons, the following layer **P+1** contain **Z** neurons then to calculate weight matrix will be **Y** by **Z** matrix.

2) Bias

In the decision-making process, individuals think of different factors before making the final decision. The outcomes of the decision settled upon are also mitigated. With all this thinking, some results are never expected. This is where Bias comes to use in neural networks. Neurons that are not within the input layer contain Bias. Bias and weight are a bit similar in that they both carry value. Bias can be put in matrix formats in the column sector.

Calculations

Let the layout be called Z. The formula abbreviations are as follows

- b – the value of Bias

- x - input to the neuron

- w – the value of weights

- n – The value of inputs from next layers

- i - value between o to the incoming layers

Typically, neurons that have value during the start of calculations are the input neurons found within the input layer. To obtain the other layers neuron values one needs to;

a) Multiplying all the inbound neurons with its weight.

b) Taking the values and adding them together.

c) Then adding the bias matrix of the neuron needed.

The above calculation involves obtaining Z. This method is hectic when it consists in calculating numerous neurons. The most straightforward tactic employed to carry out the challenging part involves;

The weight matrices formed can be used.

1. A weight matrix is formed that transmits value between the input layer and the output layer; e.g. (Y) by (Z) matrix.

2. A bias matrix is also formed (Y) by 1.

3. The input layer matrix (Z) by 1 is created.

4. You are transposing the weight matrix to form (Y) by (Z) matrix.

5. The dot product is determined. This can be done by obtaining the value of transpose of the input layer and weight. The outcome of (Y) BY (Z) matrix and (Z) by 1 matrix is (Y) by 1 matrix.

6. Add the dot product to the bias matrix. The value usually comes of equal measure if the calculation is done correctly.

7. In the end, one obtains the value of the neurons (Y) by 1 matrix.

The steps above should be repeated for each weight matrix and the neuron values until the last bit to obtain the output layer.

The explained method above can only be used in a connected neural network.

Neural Networks and Learning Machines

The Neural networks are a series of algorithms programmed to solve complex computations. The idea is to make it mimic human being neurons. The artificial neural network can be used in enabling machines to learn and recognizing patterns. The system derived from this idea works by analyzing value layer inputs.

The neural net can be presented in a graph format. It's made of nodes. Arcs link the nodes. The weight brings together the nodes and the arcs. The weight within the neurons transmits the values. The network of neurons forms the machine learning program. The signals being transmitted within the neurons usually are in chemical and electrical setups. The sector can help in regression of constant target traits. A neural network can be used in different industries such as in business, forecasting, and also obtaining data.

The neural network is made up of three layers. Numerous nodes make up a layer. An activation function is carried out by the nodes.

V Input layer – this layer involves the raw data collected and inserted into the grid. The input layer obtains value containing instructive units. The total sum of nodes found in an input layer usually tallies with informative units. Signals and information transmitted within the nodes do not encounter any distortion in the process. Duplication of values received then happens as it received only one signal. The duplicated data is transferred to its numerous output units.

V Hidden layer – it involves the process involved in input value and the weight value obtained in the unknown entities. The hidden layer can be more than one. The weights usually increase values within the hidden layer.

V Output layer – this layer can be determined by the events ongoing on the weights and the hidden layer units and also the output entities. Output layer connects to the hidden layer. When a value reaches this layer, it's returned with a value matching its forecast unit.

Types of Neural Network

There are various types of neural networks. Models that are easy are ones made their units are connected by two layers, namely output, and input. The output and input layers' units correspond to each other.

a) Feedforward Neural Network

This type of artificial neural network is the simplest in all the different types. The data in this layer transmitted singly. Data being transmitted goes through input nodes and leaves through the output nodes. Some Feedforward Neural networks contain in them hidden layers, while others don't. The propagation in this network forward-facing.

The calculations involved the addition of value inputs and weighted value to the output layer. Reflection of the output is only done if it has surpassed a definite amount which enables neurons to be activated or not to be activated in the process.

The Feedforward neural networks can be applied in the fields of visualization in processors and communication recognition in cases whereby the act found to be complicated. Its advantage is that it has low conservation level.

b) Radial basis function Neural Network

The Radial basis functions neural network is programmed to contemplate on issues involving the space of a plug. The center of the said plug is also factored. It's made up of two layers.

It uses the Euclidean model to calculate the distances involved. The radius is obtained to help in categorizing different levels. Where the point is not within the radius, then chances of a new position being categorized is low.

Its application involves being used in energy restoration grid. The energy sector has grown, and with this comes, complications such as electric blackouts. With many people and industry depending on power, restoration needs to take place fast.

The process of blackout restoration involves the following;

- It's usually the hospitals, institutions, police stations and also essential infrastructure such as train services that are considered first. Before any other clients, when power is being restored.

- The next step involves power stations that supply power to a large area.

- After essential clients, then power can be restored in households and estates.

Recurrent Neural Network

The response of an event is forecasted by the neural network saving the output layer then transmitting this data to the input layer.

With each step passed the neuron can remember a bit of data along the way, making it resemble a memory cell. The data collected is stored for some time to be used later. When the forecast is not right, two methods are applied to make the corrections, namely; error correction and learning rate. With these methods, the neural network makes amends to where it was wrong and begin to predict the correct assessment.

Recurrent Neural Networks can be applied in different sectors. For instance, in a text to speech adaptation. The deep voice was created through this neural network.

d) Convolutional Neural Network

Convolutional neural networks have parallel features to feed-forward neural networks. The Bias and weighted value in the neurons are directly proportional. The neural network is typically used image and motion processing.

The input variables are transmitted in the form of groups. The categorization process configured such that the neural network can recollect the images sent and more accessible computation. The operations being carried out comprises of HSI scale to Grayscale or RGB to Grayscale. The process involved help the input features are taken in batch-wise like a filter. This will help the network to remember the images in parts and can compute the operations. These computations involve the conversion of the image pixel format from RGB or HSI scale to Gray-scale. The format transformations make the program to be able to detect images. Classification can after that happen.

e) Modular Neural Network

This artificial neural network is different from the other systems, and this is because the modular neural net is made of various networks that are operating unconventionally yet adding to the output of the network. The various neural networks found within the modular system have different characteristics making the input. The subnetworks are not submitting electric or chemical signals to each other nodes while carrying out its functions. The modular neural network is preferred to other networks due to its ability to deconstruct immense computational. These allow for the complex task to be handled with ease. The process carried out improves the quality of computation by ensuring the nodes transmit faster. Amount of neurons involved will also determine the speed and quality. This kind of network has seen an increasing level of research done to be able to understand it more.

Steps one can take to build a Neural Network

1) Collecting data for training

One needs to receive a lot of data. Below are ways the neural network can be able to adapt to the pattern. The values are named A and B.

a = np. array([-2.0, 1.0, 2.0, 3.0, 4.0, 5.0])

b = np. array([-4.0, -2.0, 1.0, 4.0, 6.0, 8.0])

2) Construct the neural network

To be able to build the neural network model one needs to choose on the number of neurons and layers they want to build.

- model = tf.keras.Sequential()

- model = add (tf.keras.layers.Dense (units=1, inputs_shape= (1)

- model.summary

3) Model compilation

In this step, one chooses the type of algorithms needed, such as optimizer. The neural network will also require the loss function.

Model.compile (optimizer= 'sgd', loss= 'mean_squared_error')

4) Enter the training data collected

The data that is fed into the model will enable the neural network to search for a corresponding function. The number of connections to be made by the built neural network is to be decided.

Model.fit(a, b, epochs= 500)

5) Test the model

The built neural model, when completed, needs a test. This can be done by exposing the model to raw data. For the neural model to the considered a success, it needs to speculate the new data output precisely.

Human Brain Vs. Neural Networks

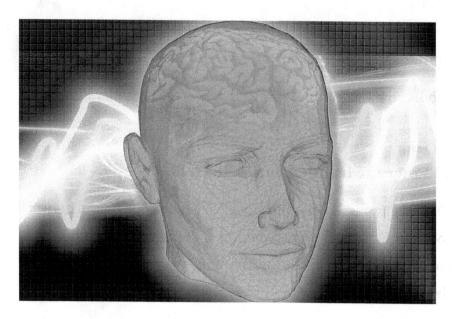

Level of Creativity

Creativity is usually explained as the ability of someone or something to develop concepts that are new or coming up with systematic models that constructive.

In the modern era, people are findings ways to develop technologies that are considered creative. The computers itself applying creativity in industries. With this, computers have been able to challenge some scientific theories, creating music beats and also developing approaches by are useful.

Computers though are not capable of knowing what the best new idea is. Modern computers haven't produced any new scientific theories, only challenging some existing ones. The human brain still has an advantage over it in this sector.

Ability to have Emotion and empathy

These two feelings of Emotion and empathy are yet to be fully comprehended by the neural networks. Emotion is an essential aspect of being able to forecast what events can happen, and it also acts as a form of controller. The level of accuracy to detect facial gestures by the neural networks has increased immensely. In the modern world, some technology companies are trying to develop robots that can provide company to people.

Process of creating a plan and executing it function

The function of Planning and executive ideas is an essential part of the human brain. This function originates from the pre-frontal lobe. The human brain frontal lobe came into existence and is found in Homo Sapiens Sapiens. The ability of the human brain to plan and execute cases of people being able to speculate on the future event and outcomes.

Human brains are less likely to make a rational decision compared to computers. While this is the case, the ability of humans to process emotions better than machines enable them to be way adaptable and better in making plans and being able to execute them. Computers are limited in carrying out this function as the speed level is not considered.

Consciousness

Consciousness is defined as the self-referential involvement of our reality and choices we make and able to feel at each particular time. It's what gives people motivation in the form of spirituality and level of surprise. Different physiology fields have tried to research and get to more about consciousness, but challenges are faced. Questions such as what it is. How did it come by? Where did it originate? What requirements are needed to reproduce it? Are asked continuously but without success.

With all these questions unanswered, the likelihood of consciousness being created in computers hasn't begun. Some scientist is of the idea of starting with cracking the emotion and execution function. Ethical challenges.

Hardware or software-based Neural Network

A lot of work has been carried out to be able to make artificial neural networks surrounding replications on the technologies. When one outlines sequential ANN simulators obtained from machines. The Intel Pentium processor is one of the neural networks which is growing exponentially due to its high-performance standard. Its form of conventional von- Neuman processor. The fastest processor though is not likely to bring about real-time reaction and the learning of the network which have a large number of neurons. The opposite happens for parallel processors with many modest processing elements.

Applications of hardware neural networks involve communication recognitions in items and also devices. The hardware neural networks can also operate a large number of orders at a faster rate compared to neural software networks.

Advantages of Artificial Neural Network

❖ Storage facility for the system- data is stored in the system such as modes of programming in the whole network. When some data goes missing, it doesn't affect the function of the net.

❖ The network can function with limited information- the moment the neural network has been feed with training data; a successful model will produce outputs even with less information. The only limiting factor is affecting the performance hinges of critical data inserted.

❖ The Artificial Neural networks are straightforward to apply.

❖ Level of tolerance for errors is high- when a particular cell in the artificial neural network gets distorted, the data output gets produced still.

❖ Memory function- the ANN can learn. This can be achieved by training the ANN by showing illustrations to the system. The proportionality of the network to the shown illustrations is direct.

- ❖ Slow distortion- the ANN gets corrupted with time although this happens slowly.

- ❖ Ability to train and Learn- the ANN can learn from examples shown and from that training able to make better choices when faced with a similar scenario.

- ❖ Parallel processing ability- the number of networks in a system can enable it to execute different functions.

The Disadvantages of Artificial Neural Networks

- ❖ Level of dependence on Hardware- the artificial neural networks depend much on processors to execute its functions properly. The processors need to behave a parallel processing power.

- ❖ Unsolved functioning of the system- the artificial neural network is not capable of explaining how and why signs when a solution is searched. This limit is the most critical in the network system.

- ❖ The level of assurance for the structure of the network to be outstanding- there are no policies put in place to regulate the kind of artificial neural network structure required. The ideal stricter is usually obtained through trial and error assessments.

❖ Reinstructing Artificial Neural networks are robust-Adding data at a later time will likely bring corrupted results.

❖ The challenges faced to give an illustration of problems to the neural network model- the most challenging part is converting problems into numerical values before feeding to the artificial neural network. The ANN only absorb data in a binary format. The accuracy of the model working well in this case all depends on the ability of the user to convert useful data.

❖ The period of network function is relatively unknown- the ANN system sometimes comes up with error as a value which is a limit.

CHAPTER 5: PREDICTIVE MODELLING

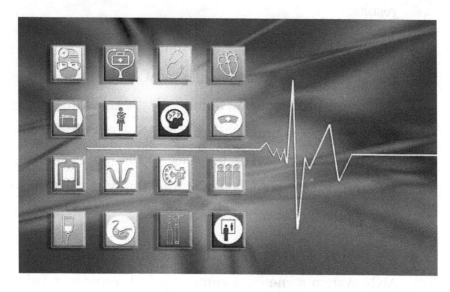

"Science is a little bit more than a wonderful way of modelling and predicting; it's a wonderful technical abstraction. I think science is a really wonderful technical abstraction"

Bernard Beckett

Predictive modelling is a tool used in Predictive analytics in a process that includes already collected/tabulated data from the past or current to draw future outcomes. It involves a data mining process that tends to forecast the possibility of getting new results or remain the same in the future.

Once data is collected, a statistical model is created to help make the predictions/ guesses on a future trend or behaviour related to certain data at hand. For example, growth in technology. With the recent trend of social media use, they can use the numbers or data from phones, web searches and so on to predict the data and come up with an assumption of what will happen for like the next ten years. This helps in deriving changes or solutions to solve the issue or improve it.

So as to come up with the right value or results for the future, the statistical model can be revised from time to time, adding results from other sources to better its performance.

Predictive modelling is accurate in its predictions as it gives accurate forecasts by allowing users to ask questions or make assumptions.

Predictive versus Interpretation

Predictive is about anticipating, estimating, or forecasting what may come about in the future. On the other hand, interpretation is asking a series of questions about data. It involves implementing processes in which data will be reviewed and sampled before its original outcome. They work together to ensure e data being used in the model is of the highest quality.

Techniques of Predictive Modelling

Predictive modelling involves two main techniques which include:

Regression technique

It is mostly used in statistics to find the effect of one variable has on the outcome. Using the linear regression, they can use the data to determine the Variable on the relationships these variables have to one another. By using the normal distribution, it is able to find the specific factors from a large number that affects the product. On the other hand, logistic regression, the outcome is determined based on the results of other variables which are discrete to get a prediction. It mostly follows the data from the already existing list to determine the only limited response based on a categorical number. The number is always 0 or 1 or in multiple regression where the numbers can change to 2 or 3.

Neural Networks

This technique is used as the Artificial Intelligence (AI) model to handle complex functions. They can be applied in classification, control, and prediction in different sectors of neuroscience, finance, and medicine. In this case, it works without knowing the relationship between the input and output. There need to be training, both supervised and unsupervised.

It works on the basis of Artificial Intelligence. For instance: smart assistants, image recognition, and natural Language Generation. It's a powerful model with the ability to review a huge amount of labelled data in search of correlations between variables.

Application of Predictive Modelling

Predictive modelling can be applied in different sectors and guarantee the best results. It has been used before, and it has resulted in positive results. It can be used not only in the financial institutions but also in educational organizations and businesses.

It can be easily applied in the following areas:

·   **Health**

Health sectors can use predictive modelling to determine the life expectancy of cancer patients which can help the physicians with treatment options. It can also keep the records of those patients with serious health issues and risk being admitted from time to time.

Healthcare providers can be able to predict the effectiveness of new medical procedures, medication, treatment options, and tests. This can also help them improve the health sector and predicting a healthier and improved health sector.

Moreover, hospitals can be able to monitor their patients' records or their employees. This will help them have all their data and predict their possibility of retaining their job in the next five years or monitoring the health of their patients with ease.

- **Insurance**

For the health insurers, they can be able to determine the health status of their customers and determine which of them is more at risk and needs special care. They can detect any danger with chronic illnesses as well as fraud in the health sector. Using the data of their clients, they can decide what best suits them in case they have an attack next time. They mostly rely on the medical; results in the system and get a probability of who will need a health provider to take care of them.

Insurance companies prefer it for retaining customers, determine the premium rates, and detect fraud. Insurance managers use it to grow and avoid risk by safeguarding the lives of their policyholders at any given time. For a vehicle or bike insurance, they will predict the chance of it serving you for long or any cases of accidents.

- **Customer retention**

Recently, there is a lot of competition, and ensuring your customer is satisfied and awarded should not be the case. You should not wait for the customer to complain about your products and terminate your agreement to act. You need to make sure predictive modeling as you will learn about the probability of the customer staying and what you can do as well as their behaviours.

- ## Telecommunication

They can use it to retain more customers. They can use the data on different media platforms to help create good relationships and new customers for their cross-sell/up-sell. In most cases, they concentrate on their most esteemed and valued customers.

- ## Media and entertainment

They can use it for determining trends, influencing attributes, and how the sports and entertainment sectors are fairing. They can get all the information about entertainment in different sectors easily than before, which could take an entire week to arrive at a finding. In most cases, media can negatively influence people if the content is not right for them. This greatly helps as they are able to determine appropriate audiences for a certain content without much effort.

- ## Manufacturing

For any manufacturer, you may need all the information on the production process, what is needed in terms of resources, manpower, and skills. You can predict the outcome of the product as well as determine their failures and the possible solutions to the problem. You can also use the information on making sells and targeting the right people for your products. It can guarantee you data on the quality and quantity of products you have done. That can help predict the number of products or assets you will be able to produce after a given period of time.

- **Utility companies**

It helps detect any malfunctions in the equipment used, future solutions to the problems, resources required, improve the safety of the equipment or resource and reliability as well as the risks involved. Understanding this data will predict the outcome of the problems and how to solve the issues before the case.

- **Retailer**

You can decide on matters of goods, the availability, and demand and how to grow your brand using campaigns and other marketing strategies to get customers while retaining those you already have.

- **Child protection**

The child welfare agency uses this tool to curb child abuse and neglect. In the past, there were cases of neglect and abuse, as the people involved did not face the law. Nowadays, welfare ensures that children are protected and in case they are abused, and they can report easily and get help.

- **Sports**

Sports, like any other area, has embraced the use of predictive modelling id predicting sports lineup and the possible winner. Using the information from their past games and the recent ones while comparing their strength and weaknesses could help analyse results for future tournaments or line-ups.

Predictive Modelling Process

This process involves a number of steps to make prediction easy and effective. They include the following:

1. Understand your business objectives

2. Define your modelling goals

3. Collect data

4. Prepare your data

5. Determine the required variable

6. Select and built models

7. Validate models

8. Use models

9. Monitor the performance

Predictive Modelling Tools

Predictive tools have, in recent times, become popular for giving data its meaning. Unlike in the past, where it was less used due to lack of enough skills and were restricted to IT. These tools are easier to use, and they ensure your prediction makes sense. Most business people and those from different sectors have established a relationship with these tools by developing new ones to help make prediction easier and more worthwhile. These tools help detect problems and give solutions on how well to handle the problems.

These tools are differently designed depending on your needs. There are those created for the experts, and others can be handled with anyone. These include:

·   **TIBCO Software**

It helps the brand make the right decisions basing on the data of their customers. They mostly look at the trends and behaviour of their customers and know how well to retain them. What will fit them and if they will stick for long or not?

·   **Terracotta In-Genius**

It helps organize data in an as easy and effective way. It groups the data in different categories to make prediction easy and fast.

·   **Medalogix**

This tool is used in the hospitals to make the right decisions concerning patients stay in the hospital as well as their treatment using their records.

- **MyCityWay**

It helps brands and organizations set up their mobile app to use for referrals and campaign marketing.

- **Medio platform**

They help understand the reason as to why their customers have left their website by knowing their behaviour. Mostly, it works by making the brand understand what their customers are yearning for from them.

- **SAS Text Miner**

It helps brands arrange and categorize their data in a more quickly and effective way in regards to their requirements.

Data Preparation for predictive modelling

Data preparation is an essential part of predictive modelling as it tends to clean up and select the right data for your prediction. The data to be used here should be of high quality and meets the acceptable terms.

Since the data to be used should be clean, relevant, and on point, you may need to follow these steps to ensure you have the right data for your predictive modelling:

· **Identify the data**

Once you have identified the data you need, ensure it is the one you seek as data ends to be found in different formats and styles at different sources. A source will direct you to what you need.

· **Look for ways to get the data**

Probability is that the data you need is not yours. You need to look for ways to contact the owner of the data. If its data from a raw source, you can collect it and make the right changes to make it worthwhile.

· **Decide on what variables to use in your analysis**

As you may not know which set of variables will give you the right results, you can consider using a variety of variables to determine which one actually works for you.

· **Decide whether to consider derived variables**

Ensure you use the already known variable than that which has never been used before for better results.

- **Know the data you collected**

 Knowing your data will help you determine your output. High quality and accurate data will help you get the right predictions. It will give you the clarity you need in choosing the right algorithm for your model. You should ensure your data is complete, has no errors and has no missing characters for the best service.

- **Choose the right algorithm**

Once your data has established the right relationship, it is now ready for predictions. You should note that information that does not have a relationship with the model; there will be challenges along the way.

Predictive Modelling Case Study

Predictive modelling is related t a lot more than the business world. Through its techniques, it can help come up with future solutions of an issue through prediction. Using a wide number of data from different sources, you are sure to get the best future outcome.

Here are some of the case studies of predictive modelling in:

Actuarial science

Predictive modelling related to predicted and explanatory variables. It mainly deals with financial events in the past and the present to come up with a prediction in insurance as well as other risk management applications. In matters of insurance, predictive modelling helps you understand the risks involved in the insurance sector as well as having an idea on how to save your customers from leaving.

When dealing with property and casualty insurance, you can be able to predict the cases of accidents and the casualty as well as the loss of property through fires, floods, and so on. From the prediction, you can plan for any accidents and ensure your policyholders are helped immediately they pass through property damage or accident. You will also learn of the risks involved in the process and learn t prevent it.

Drug sensitivity

Use of prediction in the treatment response of cancer patients is an important part of predictive modelling. Having their data on various treatments may help doctors make an easy decision on what kind of medication they should be given and what therapy would work for them.

It targets the types of alterations in cancer patients such as gene sequences and point mutations and their ideal therapies. Response to medication may help biologists and doctors to research on what compound is causing the reaction and how well to solve it. You will get to know of the side effects of the drug on different cell lines, humans or animals.

Drug sensitivity refers to the extreme response to treatment. Once you select the variables to be used and the research from different research, you can implement the model that will predict the outcome of the drug sensitivity either from clinical tests or research.

Marketing

Marketing can be used in predictive modelling to improve the results of the organization or business. In recent times, more business people have trusted Predictive modelling. They can use it to campaign, improve the operations in your business, and know how to retain your customers as well as getting new ones. Retaining your customers has been found to increase your profit and using the right data to predict your future could help you keep solutions in place for problems you may encounter on your way and be financially safe as you will be prepared for whatever may come.

It enables you to learn how to attract your customers and what to do to remain in a highly competitive world. You will learn to take risks to grow your business as well as give your customers what they need.

How to build a simple predictive model

A predictive model is an amazing way of coming up with the correct outcome. You use the data you have to predict the future outcome. For these results to be successful, there need to be factors that should influence the possibilities of your outcome to happen. As it involves machines to help in prediction, you need to sort data correctly to give you a perfect result. First, you have to build the model to work effectively. Here are the simple steps on how to go about it:

1. Data

For a successful predictive model, there needs to be data so as to enable the prediction. You need to collect data that can help make correct predictions. As much as the data used can be in bulk, you may have to table it well to enable the model to work on future outcomes.

2. Model

It will give us the prediction results we are looking for. It incorporates computer algorithms in coming up with the correct future outcome. It can handle a set of data to make predictions, and the moment it is built, you can be able to use to predict. The model will be used for learning and giving results.

3. Prediction

Prediction is the assumption that will be made. The date you have collected is what will be used to make predictions on the outcome you can use a different or same set of data to get results. Predictions will be made after the model algorithm is used to relate the data and make a future prediction.

Why implement Predictive Modelling?

Recently, more and more business people have embraced the use of Predictive modelling techniques to keep their growth. It is no longer a thing of the mathematicians or physicians as it has been proven effective due to their positive results in different organizations. As you need to give your computers your data to come up with a model to provide you with future outcomes; you will prepare well according to the results not to be affected negatively.

It comes with a number of benefits worth trying. For instance:

Reducing Risk

You will be able to monitor your credit scores and analyse your customers' credibility. You will be able to understand the losses you have recurred in the past and get to know how well to solve the issue in the future to avoid negative effects on your credit score.

Improving operations

Most companies may consider using predictive modeling to check their inventory as well as manage and save resources. Some use it to make its operations easy and easily accessible by their customers. For example, airlines use it to set the time for arrival and departure as well as the price. Hotels and restaurants can predict the number of guests they will receive in a day and their service; food and accommodation and table their income easily. It makes it easy for you to manage your inventory by analysing the profits and loss without looking into files.

Detect Fraud

Fraud may have a negative impact on your business. Predictive modelling allows you to detect any criminal behaviour in your business. With the increase in technology, cyberbullying is an order of the day. So as to prevent this, this process helps you spot any underlying threat and enables you to solve them on time.

Optimize Marketing Campaigns

For any business to grow, you need to invest in your marketing strategies. Predictive modelling will help you grow your business by attracting potential customers and retaining regular customers. They help determine customer responses on your products and their possible purchase.

CHAPTER 6: CYBER AND NETWORK SECURITY

"Whatever you're selling, storage or networking or security, you're going head to head with the incumbent players"

Marc Andreessen

Computer Network refers to the interconnected group of computers and other devices connected to share information. However, there are different types of network depending on the location of individual computers and devices. Firstly, there is Local Area Network (LAN), which involves a smaller geographical area like an institution. Secondly, there is Metropolitan Area Network (MAN) which involves a relatively larger area like a network that joins all the outlets of a certain organization across different cities. Lastly, there is Wide Area Network (WAN) which connects computer and devices which may be very far from each other, as in the case of the internet.

Due to the grouping of more than one computer, any unauthorized access to the system can expose much information. Similarly, an illegal penetration into the system lowers the confidentiality and authenticity of the information and the data shared or stored.

Resultantly, developers have come up with strategies that will guarantee the security of data in a network. This is through security measures such as firewalls, multilevel security system, and biometric authentication, among others.

The main aim of Network Security is to ensure confidentiality, integrity, availability, and reliability of the data stored therein by preventing unauthorized intrusion. In case a network is not secure the following can happen:

- Leakage of sensitive information which can be used to defame or, generally used against the correspondents.

- Any unauthorized person can introduce Trojan and viruses to the system. When a single component of the network is affected, chances are that any information that will be sent from the device may have the viruses which will eventually affect the whole network system.

- In case, unauthorized and malicious person gets control of the network, the saved or shared data may be altered or deleted, which can cause chaos in the corresponding institution or organization.

Short Introduction to Cyber Security

With increase in use of technology there are malicious people who will try to use it against you by gaining access to the data illegally. Most of businesses', governments', and personal activities are being carried over the internet. Businesses are sharing data from one station to another through internet or store the same in the cloud storage. The governments have initiated online processing and application of documents. At a personal level, many people are sharing information regardless of their geographical location.

Therefore if any person gets access to any of the network, there are chances of exposure of personal and sensitive information. Cyber-attacks have been a great threat to many individuals, banks, institutions, organization, and even governments.

There may be loopholes in any network, particularly when using WAN. As a result, cybersecurity is the measures placed to secure internet-connected devices, that is, hardware, software, and data, from attacks.

Attacks, in this case, means unauthorized intrusion and access of data which one is not privileged to see.

The main activities that an intruder can conduct are:

- Accessing information illegally.

- Deleting stored information.

- Modifying the data.

Cyber-Attacks and Cyber Hackers

Cyber-attack is a term that refers to any malicious intrusion that gives unauthorized person access to your information and data. On the other hand, cyber hackers are the persons who perform those criminal acts of gaining access to certain, system, data or information illegally and may decide to modify the data. Similarly, they can block the genuine user from accessing the data until the subject meets some conditions that the hackers will place.

Hackers can do the following to any data they gain access to:

Alter the Confidentiality of Information: Some information or stored data may contain confidential information about particular person. Hence unauthorized access will breach the confidentiality of the information.

Interfere with the Integrity of The Information: The second activity that hackers can do is modifying the information to work in their favour or the person behind the scene.

Interfere with Availability of the Information: Hackers can delete any information at their disposal or block the authorized from accessing the information.

The History of Cyber Security and Cyber War

Each and every day, cyber-attacks are becoming sophisticated due to increased technological advancements. As new technology emerges, hackers will eagerly work to find loopholes. Generally, there are types of cyber-attacks namely:

- Unpatched software.

- Phishing attacks.

- Trojan horses.

- Network-traveling worms.

- Advanced persistent threats.

- Denial-of-services.

Hacking and cyber-attacks have been there for long. In history, there are several occurrences of cybercrimes as recorded below.

The Morris Worm: So far, this has been regarded as the first cyber-attack which occurred in 1988. However, it is believed that Robert Tappan Morris, Cornell University graduate, started the activity with a good intention, but it ended on the wrong side. The primary intention of the program he had developed was to establish the number of computers connected to the internet. However, in the process of making the program more accurate it got installed in a computer forcefully even if the computer has had a similar installation. Eventually, it caused crashing of systems, and it is regarded as the first Denial of Service attack as it affected 10% of entire internet-connected computers of that time. Consequently, Morris was charged with violation of computer fraud and abuse act and was sentenced three years of probation and community services plus fines.

LA KIIS FM Porsche Contest: This was an intentional cyber-attack that occurred in 1995 and conducted by Paulsen. LA KIIS FM was awarding the 102nd caller a Porsche. As a result, Paulsen used his hacking abilities to claim the victory. He illegally intruded the channel's phone network and blocked their ability to receive calls; resultantly he became the 102nd caller thus emerging the winner. However, he was eventually arrested and sentenced to five years in prison.

2002 Internet Attack: In 2002, the first cyber-attack that affected the internet was recorded. The event took about an hour having targeted 13 Domain Name System (DNS) root servers. Though the Denial of Service did not affect many people, perhaps it sustained for long it could have shut down the entire internet. So far there is no recorded similar sophisticated attack.

Church of Scientology Attacks: In 2008 a group referred to as Anonymous targeted a website owned by Church of Scientology as a Denial of Services attack. The group, which was an activist movement against the church, conducted approximately 500 Denial-of-Services attacks to Scientology website in one week.

Resultantly, a Jersey teenager was sentenced two years of probation plus fines for the crime.

2013 and 2014 Yahoo Attack: Though the attack was revealed in 2016 while in a negotiation process, Yahoo was a victim of cyber-attack in 2013 and 2014. In the attack, approximately 500 million accounts were compromised in 2014. A similar attack was also recorded in 2013, where one billion user accounts were compromised. The attacks affected the value of Yahoo with approximately $ 350 million.

2014 JP Morgan Chase: In the attack, hackers gained access to names, addresses, phone numbers, and emails of approximately 76 million households and 7 small businesses accounts. However, the hackers were unable to retrieve social security numbers and passwords.

2016 Adult Friend Finder: In 2016, approximately 412.2 million accounts were attacked, exposing names, email addresses, and passwords for accounts spanning over 20 years. The hackers took advantage of weak password protection, SHA-1 hashing algorithm; as result, even passwords were exposed by the time the attack was discovered.

2017 Equifax Cyber-Attack: In 2017, hackers managed to attack approximately 143 million user accounts exposing sensitive and valuable data. The leaked data included birth dates, social security numbers, addresses, driving license numbers and some credit card numbers. Equifax announced publicly in September that they were responsible for the attack.

2018 Exactis Attack: In June 2018 unknown marketing firm leaked approximately 340 million records which made it double effects of Equifax attack. However, it was established that the cause was weak cyber-security, which made the database accessible to any hacker thus revealing personal information stored therein.

Cyber Security Certification and Laws

Regarding cybersecurity, there are different and distinct areas of specialization which include law of crime, liability, compliance, contracts, and policies. All learners are equipped with techniques such as credible preparation, giving reports in forensics, incident response or other investigations.

Global Information Assurance Certification is always awarded to learners who learn and can conduct cybersecurity processes and ensure security of firms from external attacks. Other entities in cybersecurity certification are HIPAA, GLBA, FISMA, GDPR, and PCI-DSS.

Cyber Security Engineering

Cybersecurity engineering refers to securing information, professionally, by performing activities such as designing, establishing and implementing safe network solutions to reduce the vulnerability of a network from an attack, hacking or illegal intrusion.

Most organizations hire cybersecurity engineers to, frequently check on the vulnerability of their networks from attack. The engineers can work in isolation or groups depending on the task. Therefore, cybersecurity engineers should possess expert-level understanding of how different networks operate and how activities in a network happen under normal circumstances. This will help them in identifying abnormality, which in most cases is an identifier of an attacked network.

Additionally, the engineers will have to conduct penetration tests where they can be termed as white hackers. White hat hackers work to establish the chances that a malicious black hat hacker has to intrude into the network. Therefore, an engineer in an organization has the role of testing the network, computers and application for vulnerabilities.

Similarly, all the engineers should be equipped and aware of the established laws in cybersecurity. They should comply with Gramm-Leach-Bliley, HIPAA, GDPR, PCI-DSS, data breach notice laws, and other regulations. Of equal importance, they should be aware of agreements, insurances, outsourced services, private investigation services, and also cloud computing issues.

Cryptography

Cryptography is the solution for cyber-attacks that are achieved through coding the information to make sure only the privileged have the ability to read and process it. This can be achieved through encrypting the data as the name, cryptography, 'crypt' means hidden all vaulted message while *graphy* means processing or writing.

The main aim of this branch of computer science is to ensure that the shared message is hard to decipher unless one is privileged to do so. Some encrypted message will require passwords to open them; this technique means even if the information lands in the wrong hands, it will be useless unless the recipient has the passwords. The set passwords are mostly, unique number such as national identification numbers, passport number or number that is solely associated with the recipient.

The primary goals of cryptography are:

- Ensure that the confidentiality and privacy of the data are maintained.

- Ensure that the integrity of data by making sure it remains original.

- Ensure the authentication of the sent or received data. Recipient or sender can confirm the identity of the correspondent.

Cybersecurity in the Era of AI and ML

Human beings have been regarded as more intelligent than machines, but why? The human being is able to perceive, that is taste, hear, sense, smell, and see. That is why whenever one fails to do things logically the politest response to search a person is *'Use your common sense.'* The main reason behind this is that human being has the capacity to deduce meaning from what they can perceive. However, for long computers have been regarded as having no IQ, it could not respond to climate changes or sense the mood of the day it just does as instructed.

However, artificial intelligence is the features that computer industries are incorporating in the computer to make them have equal or greater than that of human 'Intelligence Quotient.' Therefore, artificial intelligence is the characteristic of the computer that will enhance its perception and response and stop being a 'dumb machine.'

On the other hand, machine language refers to the language that a computer understands commonly referred to as codes.

Artificial Intelligence in Cybersecurity

Artificial intelligence has been established to stop the computer from being a dumb machine but an intellect machine. As a result, AI has been implemented by many organizations and also in combination with machine language it offers tools that support cybersecurity

How Artificial Intelligence and Machine Language can Anchor Cyber Security. Following are the ways that Machine language can anchor cybersecurity.

If an organization manages to detect cyber-attacks in advance, they will be able to counter the adversary from achieving the same. Machine Language as part of artificial intelligence has proven to be effective in detecting cyber threats by analyzing data. The analysis helps in spotting out of any threat and vulnerability of your information.

Through usage and adaptation of algorithms based on the data received, machine language enables the understanding of consequent improvements that are required. Through this feature, machine learning helps in proper prediction of threats by making a distinction between normal and abnormal behaviours. Therefore, when the adversary decides to launch the attack it will have been detected earlier or detected immediately, lessening the effects. Similarly, it will show specified threats which human efforts cannot detect making the computer more intelligent.

Since hackers will always keep advancing in their tactics, there are many threats to deal with daily, which at times can exceed human capabilities. However, AI is a conventional technology and will help in anchoring cybersecurity by adapting to the advancements.

On the other hand, all of the efforts should be made to make the network naturally secure through the following activities.

Using passwords and authentication protection: For any hacker to cause damage or threat to your network, they must have the access first. However, passwords have become so fragile in recent days regarding cyber security. The main causes of weakness experienced in regard to passwords are:

- Most people use similar passwords across all the accounts.

- Using similar passwords for a long time.

- Registering some sites which they are not sure about.

- Being so curious until they later learn it was bait.

In order to make sure that you are always safe at a personal and organizational level you should do the following:

- Have different passwords for different accounts.

- Update your password with time to prevent any hacker who may have reached your previous password from accessing the account and perhaps conducting denial-of-service hacking.

- Do not follow links that you are not sure about. Some links will direct you to accounts that have your sensitive data, and before you note it you will already be a victim.

On the other hand, developers are using Artificial intelligence to develop biometric authentication to replace numeric and alphanumeric passwords. Consequently, you will not need to update your passwords and using different passwords. Such features include face recognition and fingerprints.

Nevertheless, some people have referred to some of these features as irritating due fail to work perhaps when the user has changed the hairstyle the face recognition, ay take time to recognize. As a result, developers are working to innovate more intelligent devices that will overcome such challenges. According to the recent research there are one in a million chances of fooling AI particularly, through biometric authentication.

Using techniques of detecting phishing and prevention controls: Phishing is a technique that hackers use by pretending to be a genuine service provider in order to extract your security details. Researches show that one in ninety-nine unrequested email is a phishing email. Therefore, you should open only the emails you were expecting. Otherwise, a hacker can gain authority over your account.

Additionally, AI-ML has developed ways of preventing and deterring phishing attacks.

AI-ML can detect and track more than ten thousand phishing sources and respond quicker than a human being could. Similarly, Artificial Intelligence makes it possible to differentiate between legitimate and fake website in seconds unlike in human being.

Vulnerability Management: Vulnerabilities is the chances that your network has in getting attacked. However, there can be thousands of unique vulnerabilities identified yearly; this means human effort to identify such is close to impossible. However, Artificial Intelligence proactively searches for potential vulnerabilities in the system. Artificial Intelligence looks for potential vulnerabilities by combining numerous of factors such as debates in dark webs and patterns used.

As a result, AI combines the collected information to establish when and how the threat can make its effectiveness to targets.

Network Security and Artificial Intelligence: To achieve a maximum network security level, there should be creation of security policies and understanding the network topography of the given organization. While these activities can take a lot of time, Artificial intelligence learns the network traffic and suggest the most appropriate security policies.

Artificial intelligence in behavioural analytics: In most cases, the behaviour of a given network can be used to detect if there are an intrusion and modification. However, it may take time for a person to learn even the most minor activities that happen in system. As a result, implementation of AI can help in analysis of behaviour through observing pattern and algorithms, and thus it can easily detect any abnormality at its onset.

The Application of Cyber Security in Government, in Life and At Work

Hackers, particularly the black hat, are mercenaries who get access to your information; they use it for their own gain. Therefore, to avoid being victims of higher institutions and individuals with sensitive information are the most vulnerable to the attacks. As a result, cybersecurity knowledge can be used to save them from the fate. The following are the activities that will ensure a promised security of network and data at large.

1. Plan for a Unique Addresses authentication. A unique authentication makes it hard for a hacker to imitate you. For instance, AI helps in creation of biometric authentication where there is only one chance a million of personification.

2. Understand all the authentication limitations by understanding cybersecurity laws and policies.

3. Ensure your authentication can allow but also track the different geographical locations.

4. Focus on standards and results of the security measures for promising security.

5. Choose authentication processes that are not effective but not complex. The complexity of a system will make it hard for you to note abnormalities.

6. Conduct penetration tests to establish any vulnerability that your network may have for attacks.

7. Ensure privacy and installation of firewalls in your network. Similarly, use AI technology to detect phishing emails.

CHAPTER 7: LIST OF 50 KEY TERMS USED IN MACHINE LEARNING INDUSTRY AND WHAT YOU SHOULD REMEMBER

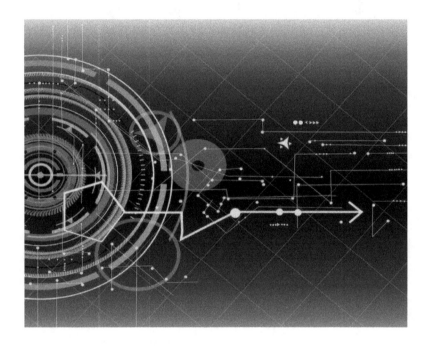

"There's a lot that machine leaning can't do that humans can do very, very well"

Diane Greene

Technology is now ruling almost every aspect of our lives. As discoveries are made nearly every day, human beings may soon have their lives controlled by technology. The concept of machine learning is an exciting field in computer science. Machine learning applies big data to develop sophisticated computer systems that can process the data and use results to predict the future. In machine learning, the computer themselves learn to process data without any prior programming. Machine learning applies specific procedures to establish patterns from a particular big data. Machine learning procedures enable industries to apply big dataset to predict future trends and manufacture products that comply with these predictions. Some of the areas using machine learning include medicine, banking, insurance and medicine. Various products have used machine learning. These include Facial Recognition used by Facebook, Siri and Cortana used for voice recognition, PayPal uses data to detect any fraud etc. Machine learning is under the field of artificial intelligence. Artificial Intelligence is the ability of machines to behave like human beings, especially in the area of knowledge and tackling problems.

Terms used in machine learning

Any field of study has various terminologies that are used. Machine learning utilizes a variety of vocabularies that are used to refer to various concepts. The following are the key concepts that are applied in machine learning:

- **Classification**- This is one of the areas of supervised learning. Supervised learning entails offering the computer the yearned for input and output data. The data submitted is easily categorized. In this regard, there are such categories like binary and decision tree. In binary classification has both a two classification and multi-classification categories. For instance, the computer can classify emails as either junk or non-junk.

- **Clustering**- This is a type of unsupervised learning that categorizes data per specific traits. You can apply the clustering method when classifying clients into various groups based on demographic knowledge. This approach will help you to target them with the right marketing messages. Multiple fields can apply the clustering method. For instance, libraries can use clustering to organize books according to titles or topics. Grouping can assist you in making an informed decision. For example, if you want to start a shoe business in a specific town, this method may assist you in understanding a location where you're likely to find clients for shoes.

- **Regression**- The term regression is used to indicate the relationships that exist between various kinds of information. Regression is under supervised machine learning. Regressions can also be used to check the correlations that exist between different sets of data. For instance, you can use the various features of a property to predict its value in real estate. There are different kinds of regression. These include Simple linear, support vector, random forest and support the tree. Within the machine learning field, regression is essential because you can apply the available data to predict the future. For instance, in medicine, a physician can use regression to predict the likelihood of a patient recovering fully from cancer.

- **Deep learning**- This term is synonyms with machine learning. Deep learning can handle big data which is unstructured the same way human beings process information. The amount of information involved is so vast that it requires many computers to handle. Deep learning, assist in data analyses and prediction of future trends. The primary application of deep learning is to detect fraud in the banking industry. There are various fields which utilize deep learning. For example, in commerce, deep learning can be applied in Chatbots and instant bidding. Deep learning is associated with particular terminologies, including:

  - ❖ **Chat box**-This program can participate in a conversation and respond accordingly just like human beings.

  - ❖ **Real-time bidding**-This algorithm assists you in purchase ads.

  - ❖ **Recommendation   engines**- Recommendation engines use the past behaviour of clients to target them with the right message. These engines use algorithms that filter data and select the one that is relevant to particular users.

- **Logistic regression**- This form of regression establishes a link between input information to forecast the resultant output factors.

- **Activation function**- The activation functions are used on layers and enable neural networks to establish complicated choice borders. **Neural Networks**-These networks resemble deep learning. They help create different layers of neurons that increase the knowledge of information derived from machines to offer error-free evaluation. Neural networks comprise of nodes which are activated to indicate the amount of significance of specific data. The neural network has three essential layers which include input, hidden and output layers.

  ✓ **Natural language processing**- This subfield of machine learning helps to analyze human speech. Through natural language processing (NLP), the computer can know, examine, control and even originate human language. Natural Language Processing helps machines to retrieve information, translation, simplify information, summarizing of data etc. There are various challenges to natural language processing. These include learning how to process extra-segmental aspects of language, the language used within specific cultures, and ambiguity in sentence construction. In machine learning, computers transform natural language into a form that is recognized and processed by a computer. Through the use of syntax and semantics, processors can analyze and interpret literature. There are various kinds of natural language processes. These include sentiment analysis, machine translation, speech recognition, semantic search etc.

✓ **Text classification-** The aim of this kind of machine learning is to forecast a label of a book. In case the documents are in a list, this method enables the system to label them according to their relevance. For instance, through text classification, you can either have spam or non-spam emails.

✓ **Sentiment analysis-** This procedure of machine learning is intended to evaluate the opinion of a client towards a service.

✓ **Document summation-** This form of machine learning helps to produce brief documents from long texts.

✓ **Speech recognition**- This is a form of machine learning that transforms audio information into textual one.

✓ **Machine translation**-through this machine learning task; a text is instantly translated from one language to another.

- **Machine vision**- This form of machine learning assists machines to recognize photos and interpret them. This type of machine learning is especially helpful in the medical field, where it can be applied to determine whether a patient has cancer. You can also use this technology to evaluate the status of traffic on the road. This technology is essential as it assists in detecting fake IDs and identifying whether the person photographed is a human being or robot. Machine vision is also useful in helping to determine the criminal found on a CCTV camera. Various aspects are essential in machine learning. These include:

- **Image classification**- Through this task, you teach a model on how to recognize the contents of a photo. For instance, you can train a design to identify an area with a disease in an x-ray image.

- **Object detection**- This machine learning model helps to train the machine to discover an object using predefined features.

- **Image segmentation**- You can teach your model to classify images using specific qualities.

- **Saliency detection**- This model will help you determine the areas of an image that viewers will pay their most attention. Saliency detection enables you to come up with high-quality adverts that target specific people.

- **Machine Learning Engineer**- This is a professional who uses data to develop computer designs that are capable of learning just like human beings. These professionals know computer technology, especially computer science and data application.

- **Machine learning**- In computer science, machine learning is a type of artificial intelligence that focuses on creating computer systems that can analyze data and give predictions. Machine learning help organizations to process big data and use the analysis to come up with products and solutions that many people want.

- **The supervised learning**- This term implies that a computer application is tutored to process specific data. The knowledge that a computer program derives from this learning enables it to come up with error-free decisions based on the information provided.

- **Unsupervised learning**- In this form of learning, the computer systems train themselves by recognizing the data given. Through unsupervised learning, models apply procedures that use unlabeled data. This form of learning assists machines to classify information according to specific characteristics. One example of unsupervised learning is clustering. Through clusters, computer models organize data in different groups. Each cluster or group has similar traits.

- **Decision tree**- This type of machine learning enables a computer to make a decision based on a graph that appears like a tree. The decision tree model allows the system to understand the repercussions of a specific decision. A decision tree is one classic example of how you can visually represent a procedure.

- **Model**- This is a representation of reality using a mathematical framework. To produce the machine learning model, you must feed your machine with a learning algorithm.

- **Generative model**- This form of the model enables the machine to produce information when you hide specific variables. Generative model in machine learning can be used to allow the business to evaluate what it requires to be efficient in offering its services.

- **Discriminative model**- This type of model is applied in machine learning to fashion the dependence on a parameter over another one, for instance, variable Y on variable X.

- **Dataset-** When you want to develop a machine learning system, you require data that you can either collect yourself or get it from particular sources. This kind of data that is applied when developing or examining an ML system is referred to as dataset. There are three forms of data set. These include training data, validation data, and test data. The training data is used to teach design. The dataset on the other hand, helps machine learning to discover patterns or decide the significant attributes for prediction. This validation design is applied to engage with different models and determining the best for your case. Specific test data is used to indicate behaviour on unused data.

- **Reinforcement learning-** This kind of learning enables the computer algorithm to play a match to reap high profits. The computer algorithm tries various games and identifies the one that enhances high rewards. The games that are commonly used under reinforcement learning include chess or Rubik's Cube.

- **Overfitting-** Overfitting implies a negative effect that comes as a result of developing a model on insufficient data. The model is biased and may not offer you accurate predictions. For instance, if you visit a butchery several times for goat meat but you don't find it, you may be annoyed. However, some so many clients are satisfied with beef that the butchery offers. In this case, you're a single person who is disappointed with the butchery's services compared to the majority of clients satisfied with its beef. In this regard, the model that you've developed is biased and does not provide with accurate and factual information.

- **Algorithm**- These are procedures that are applied in machine learning to solve problems. Algorithms help a system to process and analyze data to predict the future. There are four main kinds of algorithms. These include supervised learning, unsupervised learning, semi-supervised learning and reinforced learning. These algorithms are explained below:

- **Supervised learning**- This type of algorithm applies labelled data to learn the functions that convert input data in output data. There are two main types of supervised data. These include regression and classification data.

- **Unsupervised learning**- This form of procedure only has only input data. The two main kinds of unsupervised data include clustering and association rule learning.

- **Semi-supervised learning**- This is a combination of labelled and unlabeled data.

- **Ensemble algorithms**- This comprises of many models of weaker models with individual training to have a big prediction when they work together.

- **Training**- In machine learning training data is the initial information that helps the computer to learn to apply sophisticated technologies like neural networks to generate desired outputs. The training data comes at the beginning of the process of machine learning. After that, it is followed by validation and testing data. Training data is used to assist the computer in understanding how to process complex information, just like what happens in our brains.

- **Target**- This is what you intend to predict when you feed the computer with data.

- **Features**- These are conditions that cannot be changed that you put in your computer. Features are the main factors that are used by prediction designs to make forecasts. When evaluating features, you need to determine their attributes and dimensions.

- **Label**- A label is the real result of your target. Labels indicate the class where the information belongs. This means the different clusters of information with certain familiar features are put together for labelling.

- **Overfitting**- In machine learning, generalization is an essential factor that helps the system to predict the outcomes using the training data accurately. To enable the system to generalize explicitly, you need to ensure that the training data used is of high signal to noise ratio.

Without this accuracy, generalization will not be useful in providing accurate forecasts. A design is considered overfitting when it accurately fits in training data but is terrible in generalizing new data.

- **Regularization**- This method is used to approximate the best complexity that can be undertaken by machine learning so that to discourage the system from underfitting or overfitting issues. To reduce the independent of the design, various penalties are included in different variables of the model.

- **Machine learning Task**- This is a mixture of information with features and target. There are various kinds of machine learning tasks, including feature selection, clustering, regression, and others.

- **Prediction**- Based on specific features, the machine learning design can forecast a target value.

- **Hyperparameter**- This is a factor whose value is determined before machine learning. Various designs need different kinds of hyperparameters. However, there are those designs that do not need hyperparameters. The salient features of hyperparameters include: manually run, they are applied to assist in approximating design parameters, and they help in enhancing a model's operation.

- **Accuracy**- This is an estimation of absoluteness of a classification model. You can measure it by dividing the value of classified instances by the number of classified instances.

- **Activation function**- In deep learning activation function determines the absoluteness and the effectiveness of training design. Activation functions are represented mathematically and are applied in establishing the results of a neural network.

- **Active learning**- In this kind of machine learning, the model determines that information that it should train from. This kind of learning is essential to label data is dear to access.

- **Area Under the ROC Curve**- The initials ROC stands for Receiver Operating Characteristics. This strategy is applied when analysing the functioning of a classification design. This design utilizes a mixture of false and actual favorable rates.

- **Bagging**-Through bagging or bootstrap aggregating, you can enhance the accuracy and power of machine learning designs as applied in regression. Bagging assists in getting rid of overfitting.

- **Baseline**- This is a procedure that uses simple statistical methods and trial and error approaches to form predictions. A baseline uses basic statistics to develop forecasts of datasets. The baseline information helps users to compare the output from machine learning and the expected results.

- **Base learner-** This is a learning procedure that develops designs that are mixed by an ensemble learning design. An example of a base learner is a decision tree explained above.

- **Bias metric-** This is the value of discrepancy between what is forecast and the accurate value for recognized. There are two forms of bias metric: low bias and high bias. Low bias implies that all predictions are right. High bias, on the other hand, suggests that your design is underfitting, and you're applying an erroneous model to perform your task.

- **Deduction-** This is a method that is used to solve problems by using testing theory through observation. It uses a top-bottom approach.

- **Epoch-** This means the frequency with which the procedure deciphers all the information in a dataset.

- **Induction-** This is a problem-solving procedure that applies a bottom-up approach. You use observations to develop theories.

- **Instance-** This is a subset in a dataset. You can also use the term observation to refer to an instance.

- **Precision-** This is the ability of your design to measure positive observations. It predicts the frequency with which what is forecast is right. In case the expense of false positives is vast, precision comes in hand. For instance, if a system provides negative results when testing whether a patient has cancer, the patient will keep on incurring costs to determine the problem.

- **Artificial intelligence-** This is a subfield of computer science which is concerned with the task of creating computer systems that can collect data and analyzing it for decision making.

- **Data mining-**This is the process of analyzing big data and establishing patterns that can forecast the future.

- **Chatbot-**This is a machine program that is capable of participating in a conversation with human beings.

- **Data-** This is any information which is transformed into a digital type.

- **Genetic Algorithm-** This approach solves problems by aping the biological processes of natural selection and evolution. The design uses a random methodology to choose a pair from the universe that can act as male and female. The chances of selecting active pairs are very high. The genetic algorithm applies three kinds of rules to form a generation from the current population. These include selection laws, crossover rules and mutation laws.

- **Heuristics-** This method is applied in solving problems when the main approaches are slow. It mainly uses experiments, trial and errors, and analysis. The main advantage of heuristics over the other methods is that it is quick.

- **Natural Language Generation-** In this form of machine learning; designs are created that are capable of producing human-like language.

- **Optical Character Recognition-** This is a computer program that captures images of a text and transforms them into computable readable text.

- **Black box model-** The black-box model is a design that you can't understand by reading its parameters. The model's internal attributes are hidden.

The field of machine learning is evolving at high speed. In case you're interested in this area, you're likely to encounter various terminologies that are used. This article has highlighted and explained the critical terms used in this body of study.

CHAPTER 8: DATA MINING

"Hundreds of data-mining companies sell landlords tenant-screening reports that list past evictions and court filings"
Matthew Desmond

In this chapter, you will learn about the essential aspects of Data mining. We will talk about data mining concepts, techniques, and methods. We will also discuss how data mining is necessary for business analytics, its implementation process, as well as its importance in machine learning. Read on to find out!

What is Data Mining?

Data mining can be described as the process of sorting through vast volumes of data to identify patterns and find relationships to solve issues or problems through analyzing data. Data mining enables business enterprises to predict what is likely going to happen in the future.

It is used by companies to transform raw data into meaningful information. Businesses get to learn more about their customers to develop effective marketing strategies, reduce the production cost, and increase sales. Data mining relies on warehousing, effective data collection, and computer processing.

Data mining processes are used to create machine learning models that can be used to power applications such as website recommendation platforms and search engine technology.

How does Data Mining work? It involves analyzing and exploring large sets of data to establish meaningful patterns and trends. Data mining can be used in credit risk management, database marketing, fraud detection, and spam email filtering. We will discuss more the uses of data mining later on in the article.

Having known what Data Mining is, next, we discuss its concepts, techniques, and methods. Read on!

Data Mining Concepts

Creating a data mining model is part of bigger processes that involves everything from asking questions about the data in question to developing a model that can help analyze and answer the questions. The following six steps can clearly explain the process.

i) Defining the Problem

This is the first step in the data mining process. It includes analyzing business necessities, defining the core of the problem, defining the specific objectives for the data mining process, and defining the metrics by which the model is going to be evaluated.

To answer those questions, you will have to do a data availability study to determine the needs in relation to the available data. If the data does not support the user's needs, you will have to redefine the project. You need to put in consideration methods in which the results of models can be merged in key performance indicators that are used to determine business progress.

ii) Preparing Data

This is the second step in data mining. It is the stage where data is consolidated and cleaned. Data, in most occasions, can be scattered across an organization and stored in various formats. It may contain abnormalities like missing or incorrect entries. For instance, data might indicate that a customer purchased a product before the product was even introduced in the market.

Cleaning data isn't just about doing away with bad data or filling up missing values, it is about finding the hidden correlations in data, identifying most accurate sources of data and establishing which columns that are most fit for use in the analysis.

For data mining, you are typically working with a large set of data and can't determine each and every transaction for data quality. This will, therefore, need you to use data profiling and automated data filtering tools. Some of those tools are Microsoft SQL Server and SQL Server Data.

However, it is essential to note that the data used for data mining doesn't need to be stored in Online Analytical Processing cube.

iii) Exploring Data

This is the third stage in the data mining process. In order to make appropriate decisions when you create a mining model, you must first understand the data. Some of the exploration techniques are calculating the maximum and minimum values, calculating standard deviations and mean and exploring data distribution. Standard deviations and other distribution values can give useful information about the accuracy and stability of the results.

You can employ tools like Master Data Services to establish available sources of data and determine data mining availability. You can also use tools Data Profiler and SQL Server Data Quality Services to analyze your data distribution and repair errors like missing or wrong data.

After defining your sources, you can combine them in a Data Source by applying the Data Source View Designer in SQL.

iv) Building Models

The fourth step involves building a mining model. You will apply the knowledge you amassed in Exploring Database stage to help create and define models.

To define the columns of data you prefer to use, create a mining structure. The mining structure is connected to the source of data but doesn't have any data unless you process it. The information can be used in any kind of mining model that is based on the structure. Before structure and model processing, a data mining model is just a container that outlines the columns used for input and the parameters that tell the algorithm how to process the data.

You can also use parameters to adjust algorithms. Additionally, you can apply filters to data so as to use a subset of it, creating different results. After taking data through the model, the mining model object contains summaries that can be used for prediction.

It is important to note that whenever data changes, you should update both the mining model and the mining structure.

v) Exploring and Validating Models

This stage involves exploring the mining models, build and test their effectiveness.

Before deploying a model in a production environment, it is prudent to test how well the model performs. When building a model, you sometimes can create multiple models with various configurations and test all of them to determine which one yields the best solution to your problem.

To explore trends and patterns that the algorithms discover, use the viewers in Data Mining Designer tools. You can test how good the models create predictions by using applying tools in the designer like the lift chart and classification matrix. To determine whether the model is significant to your data or not, use the statistical technique to automatically create subsets of the data and the model against each subset.

vi) Deploying and Updating Models

This is the final step in the data mining process. This stage involves the deployment of models that performed best in a production environment. With the mining models in place, you can perform various tasks depending on your needs. Below are some of those tasks;

- Use models to create predictions that can later be used in making business decisions.

- Creating content queries to retrieve rules, statistics, or formulas from the model.

-Use integration services to create a package that the mining model is used to sort incoming data into multiple different tables intelligently.

Data Mining Techniques

Today, there are several data mining techniques used in data mining projects. We will examine those techniques in the following subsection.

Association

In this technique, a pattern is discovered based on the relationship between things in the same transaction. This is why the association technique is often referred to as a relation technique. This technique is mostly used in market analysis in order to identify the most frequently purchased set of products.

Retailers are using association techniques to discover customers buying habits based on historical sale data. This might help them establish that customers always buy a pack of crisps when they beers and they can, therefore, put crisps and beers next to each other in order to save the customer's time and in the long run, increase sales.

Classification

This is a data mining technique based on machine learning. It is used to classify each item in a set of data into one large predefined set of groups. The classification technique puts into using mathematical methods like linear programming, decision trees, neural network, and statistics. In classification, you develop software that can learn how to classify data items into groups.

Clustering

It is a data mining technique that makes use of a cluster of objects that have similar characteristics using an automatic technique. It defines the classes and categorizes objects into each class. For example, in book management in a library, there is a wide range of books each talking about different topics. The challenge in this situation can be keeping those books in such a way that readers can pick several books in a particular topic without a struggle. By using the clustering technique, you can keep books that have similarities in one shelf or cluster and label it with a relatable name. So, if readers want to pick books in that topic, they will only have to go to that shelf rather doing rounds in the entire library.

Prediction

Just as the name implies, the prediction is a data mining technique that discovers the link between independent variables and the relationship between independent and dependent variables. For example, the prediction technique can be applied in the sales to predict profits for the future if the sale can be considered as an independent variable with profit being the dependent variable. Based on the previous sale and profit data, you can draw a fitted representation curve that is used for profit prediction.

Sequential Patterns

This is a data mining technique that looks to identify similar patterns, trends, or regular events in transactional data over a business period.

In sales, establishing patterns can help businesses identify a set of items that customers buy together at different times. The businesses can then use the information to advise customers to buy it with better deals basing on their buying frequency.

Decision Trees

This is one of the most used data mining technique because its model is easily understandable for users. In this technique, the root of the decision is a simple question that has several answers. Each answer results to a set of conditions that help you determine the data that you can base your final decision on.

Data Mining Methods

There are several methods of data mining and data collection. Below, we discuss the most common methods of data mining and how they work.

I)Anomaly detection

This can be used to determine something is different from a regular pattern. For example, monitoring gas turbines and how you can detect anomaly to make sure the turbines are properly functioning. Sensors monitoring pressure and temperature are set up to see if anything abnormal is observed over time.

ii)Association learning

This is used to determine which things tend to occur simultaneously, either in pairs or groups. For example, it can be noted that people who buy milk often buy it break, and those that buy diapers, buy baby formula as well.

iii) Cluster detection

This is recognizing distinct groups within data, and the process is called cluster detection. Machine learning algorithms detect significantly worrying subgroups within a set of data.

iv) Classification

Unlike the case in cluster detection, classification deals with things that have labels. For example, spam filters are used to identify differences between content found in legit and spam messages. This can be done by identifying large sets of spam or email.

iv) Regression

This method is used to predict the future basing on the relationships within a data set. For example, the future engagement on the Facebook platform can be predicted based on everything in the user's history like photo tags, likes, infractions with other users, friend requests, among others.

Similarly, another example would be the relationship between income and education level to predict the future of a neighborhood. The regression method allows all the aspects and relationships within a set of data to be analyzed and then used to tell the future behavior.

Data Mining Implementation Process

As you have learned earlier, data mining process the sorting through of large sets of data, relationships and insights that lead enterprises in measuring and managing where they performance is now and predicting where it will be in future.

Large sets of data are brought in from various data sources and may be kept in different data warehouses. Data mining techniques such as artificial intelligence, machine learning and predictive modelling can be involved.

The process of mining data requires commitment. Experts agree that the data mining implementation process is the same, and should follow a prescribed path.

Discussed below are the six essential steps in the data mining implementation process.

1.Business Understanding

In this phase you must fulfill a number of things. First, it is needed you understand your business objectives clearly and discovering what your business requires in order to prosper.Next, you have to asses the situation at hand by finding the assumptions, resources, constraints and other important factors that should be considered. Then, from your business objectives, build data mining goals to realize the business objectives within the current situation. Lastly, a credible data mining plan has to be implemented to achieve both data mining and business goals. You should ensure your plan is as detailed as possible.

2.Data Understanding

This is the second stage in the data mining implementation process.It starts with initial data collection which is sourced from available data sources to help get relevant with the data. Some essential activities must be done including data integration and data load in order to make the data collection a success. Then, the 'surface' properties of the sourced data needs to be examined very carefully and reported. Later, the data needs to be analysed by answering the data mining questions which can addressed through reporting ,quarrying and visualization. Finally, data quality must be analysed by answering essential questions like "Is the data acquired complete?", "Are there any missing values in the acquired data?"

3. Data Preparation.

This process typically consumes about 90% of the period of the project. The outcome of data preparation stage is the data set. Once the available sources of data are identified, they need to be chosen, cleaned, constructed and formatted into the ideal form. The task of data exploration at a greater depth maybe be done during this phase to identify the patterns based on business understanding.

4.Modelling.

To begin with, modelling techniques have to chosen to be used for the prepared data set. Next, the test scene must be generated to determine the quality of the model. One or more models are then created on the data set prepared. Lastly, the models need to be assessed carefully involving all the stakeholders to ensure that created model meet the set business initiatives.

5. Evaluation.

In this second last phase, the model results are evaluated in relation to business objectives drafted in the first stage, new business needs may be raised due to the new patterns discovered in the model results or from different factors. Understanding the business is a vital process in data mining. The do or don't do decision must be made in this phase in order to move on the initiation phase.

6.Implementation

The information or knowledge gained through the entire data mining process needs to be showcased in a way that stakeholders can put it into use when they need it. Basing on the business requirements, the implementation phase could be as simple as creating a report or as complicated as repeating the entire data mining process across the company. In the implementation phase, the plans for deployment, monitoring and maintenance have to be created for implementation and also for future support.

Data Mining application in Business Analytics

Retail, finance, and marketing firms predominantly apply data mining in their operations. It helps create predictable vital information like target audiences, buying frequencies, and customer personality profiles. Therefore, data mining plays a crucial role in business analytics, as you will see in the next discussion.

As A Decision-Making Tool

Competitor analysis, market research, and industry studies are key in the intelligent decision-making process of any company.

In the banking sector, customer data is analyzed to determine customer behavior. While the sector has statistical tools for more automated trend analysis, data mining applications have ensured structures move to more objective analysis.

A relationship management strategy is key for every company. For corporate organizations, CRM has to work towards improving company productivity and better client relations.

Statistical and quantitative marketing techniques have been applied mainly to business analytics. Database marketing has been pivotal for most companies and has been increasing since the evolution of the Internet. Businesses can now predict product marketing models, response, and potential target audience for any product before it even launches.

Data mining has also been applied in market basket analysis. This is a trend in the retail industry that has caught productivity with globalization. This helps design a specific strategy for the layout of the store and marketing strategy of various products and events.

Data mining provides financial institutions with vital information about loans and credit reporting by creating a model for historical customers. Additionally, it enables banks to detect fraudulent card transactions hence protecting the card's owner.

In marketing campaigns, data mining plays a key role. This is because it helps identify customer response. This enables businesses to know which products are on high demand and on those that aren't.

Data mining provides customer response after a marketing campaign. This provides informational knowledge while determining customer groups.

CHAPTER 9: MORE DETAILS ABOUT DATA MINING

"Whenever the price of cryptocurrency is rallying, people start spending a lot more"

Erik Voorhees

In this digital era " Data Mining" has become a term that is widely used in different circumstances. It is a term that you will frequently encounter in business. This term is also popularly used in cryptocurrency mining and blockchain. But what is data mining? What does it entail? And how does it work? In this piece, we will tell you everything you need about data mining.

Data Mining for Masses

Data mining is best described as a discipline that involves the collection and categorizing data. It is a process in which all efforts are geared towards going through raw data, with the intent of turning into bits of useful information. How is this important? Well, in every business, various transactions are captured by the systems involved in the execution of relevant processes. This leaves a large trail of data in its raw form.

When data is in its raw form, it becomes difficult to utilize it for business improvement. This is where data mining comes in. For example, when you sign up for various programs or even a credit card, you leave a trail of data. Usually, this is meaningful information concerning your preferences, behaviors, spending habits, and interests.

People who sign up for a similar program leave this kind of information in the system. Collectively, it becomes an enormous data tank. Companies have to sift through this data and take the bits of information which could help grow their businesses. For example, if a company wants to increase its sales, there is some information in the large data pool that could be helpful. A data mining process enables the company to obtain useful data for that particular purpose.

Through data mining, companies decipher specific customer's traits and patterns. These patterns are then used to shape up effective business strategies. This is how companies improve their service delivery processes to meet their customers' needs.

Techniques Used in Data Mining

Four common techniques are used in data mining. These are;

1. Regression- best described as predictive.

2. Association Rule Discovery- descriptive.

3. Classification-predictive

4. Clustering-predictive.

This list is not exhaustive as there are more data mining techniques used across all industries.

Data mining tools

When data is collected, it is held in the company's database. Later, it is retrieved during the mining process. Powerful computing devices are used to access these databases during the mining process.

Besides computers, other tools are required to make the data mining process successful. Since the data is amassed in computer hard drives, software's are some of the tools used in data mining. Why are these tools needed? Data warehouses are vast and hold tons of complex information. For this reason, tools are required to sift through the data and categorize it.

This is a difficult time-consuming task. A group of individuals can't possibly single-handedly extract and analyze all the data manually. Therefore, tools are used to extract as well as convert the data into comprehensible structures. This makes it ready for future use.

Here is a list of top data mining tools and applications:

1. Rapid Miner

Rapid Miner is one of the most coveted tools in data mining. It is made by a company that goes by the same name. The developers of this software used JAVA programming language to write it. It is a powerful tool that provides clients with numerous possibilities in data mining.

Rapid Miner is best described as predictive analysis software. It provides a combined environment for text mining, deep learning, and machine learning. This tool can be used for data mining in different fields. These include business applications, research, medicine, education, training, commercial applications, and application development.

Rapid Miner has three modules. These are;

1.   Rapid Miner studio

2.   Rapid Miner Server

3.   Rapid Miner Radoop

Rapid Miner Studio handles tasks related to prototyping, validation, and workflow. Once the predictive data models are created, the Rapid Miner Server is tasked with operating them. These models are created in the studio module. Rapid Miner Radoop then breaks the models down resulting in predictive analysis.

2. Weka

This is free software, that's popularly referred to as the Waikato Environment. Weka is a machine learning software that was developed at New Zealand's prestigious Waikato University. It performs best in predictive modeling and data analysis. Some of its outstanding features include visualizations tools and algorithms. These are extraordinary features tasked with supporting machine learning.

Weka software is also written in JAVA programming language. It comes with the Graphical User Interface that enhances flawless access to its other features.

With Weka software, you can perform multiple data mining activities. The major ones include data mining, regression, visualizations, and processing. Its working principle assumes that data is organized as a flat-file. Additionally, this software can process data feedback that is returned by the relevant query.

3. Sisense

Unlike the other software, Sisense is in the category of licensed BI data mining software. It's an incredible reporting tool within an organization. This software is a product of a company that goes by the same name. It handles and processes data exceptionally well. Large and small companies can use this tool for all their data mining needs.

With Sisense, a company can combine data from different sources, and still generate satisfactory results. This software is revered for its superb visuals in reporting. Sisense is user-friendly. A non-technical staff member can use it without encountering any technical difficulties. As part of its design, it offers widgets as well as drag- and -drop options.

Widgets come in handy, especially when you want your results to be expressed as pie charts, bar graphs, line graphs and so on.

4. Oracle Data Mining

Oracle Data Mining is classified as proprietary license program. It offers outstanding mining algorithms. These are algorithms that makes it an excellent tool for specialized analytics, regression, and prediction. It is a multifaceted software used by companies to predict, target customers, and even detects fraud.

The graphical user interface of this software offers the drag and drop option. It generates the best insight in various mining activities.

5. Data Melt

Data Melt software is popularly referred to as Smelt. It is classified as an open-source data mining software. The main strengths of this software lie in visualizations and computations. It is more ideal for students, engineers, and scientists.

Dmelt is designed to be multi-platform software written in JAVA programming language. You can run it on all operating systems as long as they are in sync with Java Virtual Machine.

It is suitable for stat analysis, massive data volume analysis, and data mining. Dmelt is mostly used in financial markets analysis, engineering, and natural sciences.

6. Orange

The Orange software is preferred by many professionals in data mining. It's a good choice for data visualization. It is written in Python computing language. This component-based software is endowed with components that are known as widgets. The widgets cover data visualization and predictive modeling.

Unlike many other mining tools, Orange has an interactive user interface that takes out the dullness out of the rigorous data mining process. Also, this software formats data into desirable patterns quickly. One can move data through a simple procedure that involves flipping its widgets.

7. KNIME

KNIME is a product of KNIME.com. Its best functions include reporting and integrating data. KNIME's principle of operation is known as modular data pipeline. This software combines various data mining components with machine learning.

The pharmaceutical industry is popular with this software. It also suits companies that are interested in business intelligence, financial data analysis, and customer analysis. Since it is not a complex data mining use, people without a high technical ability can use it.

8. IBM SPSS Modeler

IBM SPSS Modeler availability is on a proprietary license. This is a product of IBM, which is a reputable global firm. It is a data mining tool that's known for text analytics and building predictive models. One of its exceptional features is the visual interface. Users need not use programming as they are already provided with capable algorithms. This qualifies as a user-friendly data mining software.

It comes with the premium and professional models. The premium model offers insightful additional features for advanced activities.

Data Mining Examples

1. Marketing

Companies are always looking for ways to segments their market, target customers, and increases sales. Data mining is deployed in search scenarios to help a company obtain certain information. This could be the age, gender, and customer habits.

The business then uses this information to their advantage. Data mining categorizes their customers is such a way that they can know who target. Once that's determined, a company comes up with promotion ideas that can appeal to the potential customers in a particular market.

This helps them deploy marketing campaigns to the right people with the hope of getting a massive response. If done right, a company can widen its customer base.

2. Banking

This is another great example of data mining. Banks are extremely interested in understanding the risks in various markets. Such information is instrumental to credit rating as well anti-fraud system. The kind of analysis that banks are out to get may revolve around financial data, card transactions, and purchasing habits.

3. Data Mining Is Essential in Day to Day Operations of Banks. It helps them determine how to get the best response

from their marketing campaigns. Data mining also helps identify the offers that customers love most.

4. Service Providers

Finding loyal customers can be difficult for service providers. It is imperative to predict how likely customers are likely to change vendors. This is a type of analysis are accomplished through data mining. For this reason, service providers have a knack for keeping large customer databases.

They collect customer's information, such as billing details, website visits, and customer service records. What follows is giving each customer score in regards to these traits. The score indicates the probability of customer switching to other brands.

Gathering this information is instrumental in retaining these customers who are likely to live. Once the customers with a high risk of living are identified, the company has to come with a way of incentivizing them. The main objective of these efforts is to make the customers stay.

5. Retail Stores and Supermarkets

Business owners who run retail stores and supermarkets are keen to know the taste and preferences of customers. With such information in their hands, they know which items to stock, and in which sizes, and at what price. What's surprising is that this data helps them understand you as a customer, more than you know yourself.

With this data, customers are classified in RFM (recency, frequency, monetary). What does this mean? It means that retail enterprises can identify high spending customers, those who may spend a lot of money one in a while, and those who spend small amounts frequently. Such information is then used to create customer offers.

6. Crime Prevention Agencies

Data mining goes beyond business. Crime prevention agencies use to minimize criminal activities. They seek to determine the trends of criminals. What they will be trying to find out is which areas are most affected, what time does the criminal take activities in most cases and so on.

After thorough analysis, they can accurately predict where and when the crime is most likely to take place. Instead of deploying security personnel haphazardly, crime prevention agencies can pinpoint the areas where more security is required.

Data mining is used in borders. It helps immigration officers to know who to search on border crossings. The parameters will be something the age or type of car being used, how many occupants are it as well as their ages.

7. Medicine

The other brilliant illustration of data mining in medicine. It revolves around patient's records, treatment patterns, frequency of ill health, and physical examinations. Medical practitioners rely on this data to administer better treatment.

Health resources also need to be managed. This entails in examining certain health risks and identifying and predicting illnesses that affect people from a certain group.

8. Tv and Radio

The media is dependent on data mining. The network wants to understand its audience much better. Moreover, data mining is important in scheduling airing of programs. Different audiences have to be targeted in distinct ways.

For instance, radios know what to air early in the morning as folks drive to work. They can tell who is likely to be listening in at that time. The same case applies to viewers. This data is valuable as it helps them decide when to air advertisements on behalf of their clients.

9. Machine learning and Artificial Intelligence

Artificial intelligence and Machine learning are becoming more important in today's world. Both of them are data-oriented. Therefore, data mining plays a huge role in each one of them. The recommendation program is an excellent example of both AI and Machine learning.

When you buy something from particular websites, other complimentary products are automatically recommended for you by the system in place. How does the system decide on the products to recommend? Data mining is the masterminding process behind all of it. This happens through analysis. It could b through studying your habits of spending, interests, and other traits.

A probability of what you are likely to buy next is established through data mining. Appropriate products are then automatically recommended for you. The same formulae are applied on YouTube, Netflix, and Spotify.

Cryptocurrency Mining and Blockchain

Cryptocurrency has continued to grow in popularity over the last few years. Usually, when users transact, these transactions between various users have to be verified. After the verification process, the transactions are added to what is known as a blockchain digital ledger. This an expanding list of records available to the public.

How Does Cryptocurrency Mining Work?

It starts with a miner. This is a node within the network responsible for collecting transactions and arranging them into blocks. Once transactions are made between users, network nodes collect and verify them. Miner nodes consolidate these transactions into what is known as a candidate block.

This process facilitates the creation of coins from these transactions. This particular coin creation transaction is known as the coin base.

What's There to Gain for Miners?

In the cryptocurrency mining process, miners are issued with a reward each time they add a fresh transaction to a blockchain.

What Tools Are Used in Cryptocurrency Mining?

Cryptocurrency currency mining is similar to other data mining processes. This means that the software's are the main tools used in the mining process. Here are some of the most popular cryptocurrency mining tools:

- GGMiner

- Minergate

- Nicehash

- Electroneum

- CGminer

Data mining plays a huge role in today's world. Government agencies and business organizations all over the world rely on data mining, to analyze, categorize, and predict. Data mining continues to evolve, helping businesses better their services, reach more customers, and strengthen improve marketing strategies. It is a phenomenon that the government and businesses can't afford to avoid.

CONCLUSION

My sincere appreciation for making it through to the end of MACHINE LEARNING FOR BEGINNERS: *Easy Guide of ML, Deep Learning, Data Analytics and Cyber Security in practice. Modern approach of Neural Networks, Predictive Modeling and Data Mining with 50 Key Terms.*

I hope that it was educational and stimulating, fluid to read and was able to provide you with the basic knowledge you need to understand the concepts of Machine Learning. By ending this guide, you will be able to understand the role of Machine Learning in influencing human behaviors in different facets of life and what deep impact it will produce in all business sectors.

We have gone through the fundamentals, basics, applications and types of machine learning. The intent of this guide was to provide you practical and effective definition of conceptions that are crucial in understanding Machine Learning.

To enrich this guide we insert a list of 50 most important terms you should know, we hope it can help you to fix the technical words.

You are now familiar of the key terms and applications of Machine learning. We are sure it will help you to find out how it works. With this knowledge you can further learn the more opportunities that exist in such technology.

Ultimately, if you found this book useful and stimulant in any way, a review on Amazon is always appreciated!